D1218742

AMERICAN ISSUES

# Freedom of Speech

*Gerald Leinwand, Ph.D.*

Produced by the Philip Lief Group, Inc.

Facts On File
New York • Oxford

Freedom of Speech



| Facts On File, Inc. | Facts On File Limited |
|---|---|
| 460 Park Avenue South | Collins Street |
| New York, NY 10016 | Oxford OX4 1XJ |
| USA | United Kingdom |

**Library of Congress Cataloging-in-Publication Data**

Leinwand, Gerald.
Freedom of speech / Gerald Leinwand.
p. cm. — (American issues series)
Includes bibliographical references (p. ) and index.
Summary: Examines the origins of the concept of civil liberties and reviews the controversial issue of what kinds of speech and expression are protected under provisions of the First Amendment.
ISBN 0-8160-2101-5
1. Freedom of speech—United States—Juvenile literature.
[1. Freedom of speech.] I. Title. II. Series: American issues (New York, N.Y.)
KF4772.Z9L45 1990
342.73'0853—dc 20
[347. 302853] 90-13914

A British CIP catalogue record for this book is available from the British Library.

Facts On File books are available at special discounts when purchased in bulk quantities for businesses, associations, institutions or sales promotions. Please call our Special Sales Department in New York at 212/683-2244 (dial 800/322-8755 except in NY, AK or HI) or in Oxford at 865/728399.

Jacket design by Catherine Hyman
Composition by Facts On File, Inc.
Manufactured by The Maple-Vail Book Manufacturing Group
Printed in the United States of America

10 9 8 7 6 5 4 3 2 1

This book is printed in acid-free paper.

# CONTENTS

# PREFACE

If people were angels, government would not be necessary. It is because men and women are not angels that government is essential. The Constitution of the United States strives to achieve a balance between governing too little and too much.

The Bill of Rights, embodied in the first 10 amendments to the Constitution, was adopted to lighten the heavy hand of government on the backs of the people. To use another metaphor, the Bill of Rights may be thought of as a traffic signal telling government when it must stop and how far it may go in controlling the freedom of its citizens. Standing at the crossroads of freedom is the United States Supreme Court. It is responsible for guarding against governmental abuse of power, sometimes halting what government plans to do and sometimes supporting what it feels it must do.

This is a delicate and sensitive role because the paradox of freedom is that freedom for you means loss of freedom for me. In the abstract, "freedom" does not exist because it is impossible for all freedoms to be approved all the time. Every time a demand for freedom is made, it is made at the expense of your own or someone else's liberty. One person's freedom ends where the next person's freedom begins. Your freedom to swing your arm ends where the next person's nose begins!

If a democratic form of government is to succeed, freedom needs to be accompanied by a sense of civic responsibility. Freedom of expression involves the responsibility to seek and speak and write the truth. Moreover, democracies require of citizens a greater tolerance for political diversity than do other forms of government. Lest the freedoms protected by the First Amendment atrophy from indifference or disuse, they must be probed anew by each succeeding generation.

It is sometimes said that had Jefferson been able to visualize that freedom of expression would extend to radio, television and satellite-guided telecommunications, he may not have been so eager to endorse the First Amendment. Yet the commanding presence of freedom of expression in the hierarchy of American values must be well understood because an important issue for the next century will be how to apply First Amendment protections in a new technological environment.

Gerald Leinwand
New York, N.Y.

# CHAPTER ONE

# Free Speech Today

*"Congress shall make no law respecting an establishment of religion, or prohibiting the free exercise thereof; or abridging the freedom of speech, or of the press; or the right of the people peaceably to assemble and to petition the government for a redress of grievances."*

Amendment I,
U.S. Constitution

Outside the 1984 Republican National Convention in Dallas, Texas, Gregory Lee Johnson, a member of the Revolutionary Communist Youth Brigade, set fire to a United States flag to protest the actions of the United States government. Arrested by Dallas police, Mr. Johnson was convicted under a Texas law that classified the flag as a "venerated object that permits criminal prosecution of those who desecrate it." He was sentenced to a year in jail and fined $2,000.

Mr. Johnson brought his case to the Texas Criminal Appeals Court. That court decided that he had been wrongly convicted—not because he was innocent of setting the flag on fire but because the law that he was convicted under was itself invalid. The appeals court felt that the First Amendment of the Bill of Rights protected Mr. Johnson because his act was a form of speech and as such could not be illegal. The Texas state law, therefore, was unconstitutional.

But the matter did not end there. The district attorney for Dallas County, John Vance, challenged the appeals court decision by bringing the case to the highest court in the nation, the United States Supreme Court. Mr. Vance, who believed that the flag represented the principles for which the United States stands, felt it should be protected against such destruction. The state of Texas should be allowed, said Mr. Vance, to make a law abridging the right of anyone to destroy the American flag.

In the summer of 1989, the Supreme Court ruled that Mr. Johnson did, indeed, have the right to make a political statement by burning the American flag. Justice William Brennan wrote, "If there is a bedrock principle underlying the First Amendment, it is that the Government may not prohibit the expression of an idea simply because society finds the idea itself offensive or disagreeable."

The decision by the Supreme Court to strike down the Texas law was not easily reached. Four of the nine Supreme Court justices disagreed with the decision. One dissenter, Justice John Paul Stevens, expressed a different point of view. He wrote, "The ideas of liberty and equality have been an irresistible force in motivating leaders like Patrick Henry, Susan B. Anthony, and Abraham Lincoln, school teachers like Nathan Hale and Booker T. Washington, the Philippine Scouts who fought at Baatan, and the soldiers who scaled the bluff at Omaha Beach. If those ideas are worth fighting for—and our history demonstrates that they are—it cannot be true that the flag that uniquely symbolizes their power is not itself worthy of protection from unnecessary desecration."

The controversy over flag burning divides the nation as well. On one side of the issue are those who feel, as did the majority of the Supreme Court, that Mr. Johnson's right to make a political statement is more important than the protection of the flag. If such a right is taken away in the instance of the flag burning, might there come a time when other forms of political speech—wearing armbands, picketing or publishing Communist pamphlets—are denied? Limiting free speech sets a bad precedent, according to this view, because to deem one action or type of speech unacceptable makes it easier to find other similarly offensive actions unacceptable, too.

On the other side of the issue are those who feel that the right of free speech should have limits and that burning the American flag should be one of them. Throughout the world, the burning of a flag is regarded as one of the ugliest, most offensive forms of antigovernment feeling. Some people, including Supreme Court Chief Justice William Rehnquist, don't even consider it to be a form of expression but instead, in Rehnquist's words, "the equivalent of an inarticulate grunt or roar." He went on to say, "Surely one of the high purposes of a democratic society is to legislate against conduct that is regarded as evil and profoundly offensive to the majority of people."

The heat of public passion over this issue ignited the action of the Congress. Following a second U.S. Supreme Court decision supporting flag burning as a legitimate form of freedom of expression, demands were again heard for a Constitutional amendment. However, on June 21, 1990 a vote in the House of Representatives fell short of the two-thirds majority needed to set the amendment process in motion. For the time being, at least, the amendment proposal is dormant.

Flag burning was not the only free-speech issue confronted by the American public during the 1980s. Incidents of book banning more than tripled from 1980 to 1989. Government censorship of television and radio shows also increased—more than a dozen radio stations and one television station were fined, investigated or formally censored by the Federal Communications Commission. Controversy over obscenity in rock music, art exhibitions and films also flourished in the 1980s, fueled by concerned parents, teachers and government officials.

Today, the channels of communication are more numerous than ever before. When our country was founded, print and live speech were the major modes of communication. Now FAX machines, compact discs, computer printouts, cable television and videos flood the American way of life with more and more information. Meanwhile, students still demonstrate on campuses, labor unions still strike and hold picket lines, and artists still push at the limits of public morality with paintings, plays and photographs that offend. Defining the limits of free speech has always been and continues to be a challenge to our democracy.

## Democracy and Free Speech

In the ringing words of the Declaration of Independence, among the self-evident truths are that "... all men are created equal; that they are endowed by their creator with certain unalienable rights, that among these are life, liberty, and the pursuit of happiness." The Founding Fathers who drafted the Constitution in 1787 reiterated the essential purpose of government in the Preamble to the U.S. Constitution: "We the people of the United States ... in order to secure the blessings of Liberty ... establish this constitution for the United States of America."

The unalienable rights and liberties to which these two documents refer are commonly known as "civil rights" and "civil liberties." Often used interchangeably, there is, in fact, a subtle difference between the two terms. A civil liberty involves the protection of an individual from government action, while a civil right is granted to an individual by law. In other words, the right to speak freely is a civil liberty, while the right to give a speech in a public park is a civil right. Together, civil rights and civil liberties encompass freedom of speech and religion, the rights of citizens to participate in the political process and the rights afforded to criminal suspects.

Perhaps the most precious civil liberty of all is the right to speak and think freely. The ability to make a choice, to judge right from wrong, to dream and imagine without limitations, are the intellectual qualities that separate us from lesser beasts. Philosophers and statesmen alike have long stressed the importance of free expression, especially in its relationship to political participation.

John Stuart Mill, a 19th-century philosopher, wrote one of history's most important and cogent defenses of free speech, *On Liberty*. To Mill, the freedom to speak one's mind freely, to discuss political and social ideas without fear of reprisals, is the key to discerning the truth: If ideas are silenced, the truth may never be known. Mill outlined three basic reasons freedom of expression should never be curtailed: (1) A censored opinion may be true and the accepted opinion false; (2) even truth needs to be challenged and tested; and (3) there is probably some degree of truth in all opinions.

According to Mill, therefore, all ideas, no matter how out of the mainstream of current thought they are, have the right to be expressed. "If all mankind minus one, were of one opinion, and only one person were of the contrary opinion, mankind would be no more justified in silencing that one person, than he, if he had the power, would be justified in silencing mankind."[1]

Another 19th-century writer who discussed the importance of free speech, especially as it related to the United States, was Alexis de Tocqueville. Sent to study America's penal system in 1831, Tocqueville, a French magistrate, published his wide-ranging observations about our fledgling democracy in the landmark book, *Democracy in America.* Like Mill, Tocqueville saw a great danger in "the tyranny of the majority," especially in the United States where "the interests of the many are to be preferred to those of the few."[2]

Indeed, perhaps more than any other system of government, it is democracy, the rule of the people, that most depends on the ability of people to make informed decisions based on free, unfettered discussion. Our society's interest in freedom of speech enables the people to participate in making decisions and in helping to choose the wisest course of action from among many possibilities.

More than 100 years after Mill and Tocqueville made their convincing observations, United States Supreme Court Justice Hugo Black reminded Americans that the freedoms secured by the First Amendment—speech, press, religion, petition and assembly—"are indispensable for the preservation of a free society." In short, freedom of speech makes democracy possible.

## Free Speech and Its Limits

When we talk about freedom of speech, we are usually talking about political speech. That is, we have a right to criticize our political leaders without punishment or fear of punishment. We can comment favorably or unfavorably on the decisions they make and on how those decisions were reached. We have a right to dissent from the view of the majority and we can say what is on our minds even though what we say may be unpopular, provocative, dangerous and even wrong.

At the same time, liberal democratic societies have always placed limits on what can be said in the public arena. In ancient Greece, where the idea of democracy was first born, a number of conditions were placed on those who wished to speak out against the government. While all citizens were given the right of free speech, the term *citizen* excluded nearly 60% of the population. Males under 18 years of age did not have the right to address the political assembly, and neither did women, resident aliens or slaves.

Another restriction on free speech born in ancient Greece and still practiced today is the concept of slander (speaking evil). In 549 B.C., one could be fined for "speaking evil of the dead" or of the living "if uttered in temples or during festivals." Calling someone a murderer or a coward in battle was also a punishable offense.[3]

One could also be punished for attempting to overthrow the democratic government of which Athenians were so proud. Legislation was enacted to punish speakers who proposed measures that the political assembly deemed as "deceiving the people, giving bad advice or promoting inexpedient or unconstitutional legislation." In effect, the Greeks recognized that while freedom to speak was central to their idea of proper government, *unlimited* freedom of speech posed a threat to the preservation of social order.

The debate over who could speak, what could be said, and in what manner ideas could be communicated would continue for centuries. Such issues are still at the forefront of civil liberty discussions in the United States today.

## English Antecedents

The modern concept of freedom of speech as a civil liberty has its root in the Magna Carta, one of the most important documents in the development of democratic government. Written in England in 1215, the Magna Carta is now recognized as the foundation of constitutional liberty for both England and the United States. While freedom of speech, per se, was not explicitly mentioned in the document, the concept of personal and political liberty was elucidated for the first time in modern history. Under the Great Charter, men could not be deprived of life or property without due process of law, and "all men in our kingdom have and hold all the foresaid liberties, rights and concessions ... forever."[4]

Despite the Magna Carta's implicit limits on government, speaking out against the monarch of England remained a risky business for centuries. Kings and church officials were the only people who were free to speak their minds; under the Tudor and Stuart rulers (1485–1688) freedom of speech, press and assembly were virtually unknown. The price one paid for opposing the Crown was imprisonment in London Tower or the loss of one's head.

When William Caxton brought the first printing press to England in 1476, the struggle intensified. The monarchs at once sought to bring this new threat to their sovereignty under their control. They decreed that nothing could be printed or distributed without prior approval by an agency of the king. Printing presses had to be licensed, and the fewer licensed the better. Known as prior restraint, such practices mean that the public has no chance to read or listen to ideas not deemed appropriate by the government. In a democracy, prior restraint is the basic enemy of free speech, because the purpose of the press is to monitor the actions of the government and keep the public informed.

Under Tudor and Stuart rule, those who secretly printed materials without a license could be punished by being whipped, pilloried or killed. In 1579, a critic of Queen Elizabeth had his right hand chopped off at the wrist so that he could no longer "use or exercise the Art or Mysteries of Printing."

Gradually, however, as the power of the Crown declined and that of Parliament grew, prior censorship of the press came under increased criticism. A powerful spokesman against prior restraint was John Milton, a famous English writer and statesman. In 1644, he published an essay that eloquently explained the dangers of a government strong enough to suppress all criticism. Foreshadowing the work of Mill and Tocqueville, Milton believed that censorship inhibits learning and weakens the argument oNf those who censor.

"Let [Truth] and Falsehood grapple;" wrote Milton in his essay, *Areopagitica,* "who ever knew Truth put to the worse in a free and open encounter?" In addition, Milton added an important element to his argument, one that is still invoked against censorship today: Who is educated and fair enough to be a censor? Who is to judge what is appropriate and what is not?

Toward the end of the 17th century, during a period known as the Glorious Revolution, ideas about free speech continued to develop. An important milestone was the English Bill of Rights of 1689, which declared that "... the freedom of speech, and debates or proceedings in parliament, ought not to be impeached or questioned in any court or place out of parliament." This had little direct impact on the average commoner, who could still be pilloried for voicing antigovernment sentiments, but it did show that the idea of freedom of speech was now gaining a stronger hold among the educated class and becoming an integral part of the English political sensibility.

Marked by inefficiency and corruption, the licensing system eventually fell in about 1700, collapsing under its own weight as much as under the mounting criticisms leveled against it. Not quite ready to give its subjects free rein, however, Parliament imposed a tax on newspapers, journals and pamphlets. By raising costs, the Crown hoped that circulation of printed matter would be reduced. If the government couldn't stop information from being printed, it could try to keep the number of people who read it to a minimum.

Meanwhile, politically and academically sophisticated communities had formed across the Atlantic in the English colonies in America. Questions about freedom of speech and the press were as heated there as they were back in the Old World.

## Free Speech in Colonial America

When the first printing press came to Massachusetts Bay Colony in 1639, the practice of licensing printers came with it. Any colonist wishing to publish a newspaper had to have prior approval from the government back in England. When licensing was replaced by a heavy tax on printed materials in England, colonial publications were not exempt—especially as they grew more and more rebellious.

The colonists protested vigorously against the Stamp Act, as the tax on printed matter was called. It was not the first time, and certainly not the last, that the well-educated and politically astute members of colonial governments would rebel against laws passed in England but applied with force in the colonies.

Since 1606, when the first colonial charter had been granted by King James and the British parliament to the colonial governor of Virginia, the colonies had been developing their own uniquely American system of government, a mixture of English common law and a new brand of representative democracy. Perhaps the most important line in Virginia's charter stated that the colonists would "Have and enjoy all Liberties, Franchises, and Immunities ... to all Intents and Purposes, as if they had been abiding and born, within this our Realm of England."[5] Although the charter did not define exactly what rights and liberties the people had, it set the stage for the century-long development of the U.S. Constitution and the Bill of Rights.

Crucial to the move toward independence was the institution of representative government. At first, colonial governments were appointed by the Crown and governed from London. Then, in 1618, the Ordinances for Virginia allowed for the first time a government to be formed in the colony itself, with direct participation by the colonists. The House of Burgesses, elected in 1619, was the first American legislature; while each colony had a different charter and governmental structure, all eventually had self-governing bodies that allowed for direct participation by its citizens.

Two other important developments on the road to our own Constitution were the Fundamental Orders of Connecticut, issued in 1639, and the Massachusetts Body of Liberties of 1641. Perhaps taking on more power than the Crown meant to offer, the appointed governors and other political leaders established the New World's first two "home-grown" codes of laws to protect the individual and political rights of the colonists.

Of the two documents, the Massachusetts Body of Liberties is perhaps the more remarkable. Many of the fundamental liberties later to be protected in the federal Bill of Rights were anticipated here: equal justice for all, trial by jury and, most important to our discussion, freedom of speech and petition at public meetings.

Slowly but surely, the colonists were edging their way toward independence and the freedom to speak their minds without fear of reprisal from the distant monarch. Because they felt they were unrepresented in Parliament, "No taxation without representation" became a rallying cry of the blossoming revolutionary movement. The Stamp Act was recognized by the colonists for what it really was: "a tax on knowledge."

When the colonies chose to fight against the Stamp Act, they recalled an argument first voiced in England by Lord Coke, a British magistrate. Back in 1610, Lord Coke challenged the notion that any government, including the Crown and Parliament, was above the law. "It appears in our books," wrote Lord Coke, "that in many cases, the common law will control Acts of Parliament, and sometimes adjudge them to be utterly void: for when an Act of Parliament is against common right and reason, or repugnant, or impossible to be performed, the common law will control it, and adjudge such Act to be void."[6]

A century and a half later, the rebellious colonists read this opinion to mean that if a law is contrary to fundamental common law, it should be considered void. More specifically, if the Stamp Act denied the colonists the civil liberty of free speech, it should be repealed. The idea that government and its laws were subject to judicial review by a court would become a cornerstone of American constitutional law soon after the new nation was born.

Free speech for all was not, however, the aim of even the most rebellious colonial governments. As it had been in democratically spirited ancient Athens, free speech in the colonies usually meant free speech for those in power. At first, only high government officials and leading clergymen could speak at liberty; later, members of the legislatures could debate at will in the assembly. But it would take the drafting and enactment of the Bill of Rights in 1791 for freedom of speech for all citizens to become official government policy.

## The Drafting of the U.S. Constitution

After the American Revolution ended in 1781, the difficult task of forming a new nation began. Those who gathered in

Philadelphia to establish the structure of the government were highly educated men, men who were acutely aware of the painful struggle that their ancestors had waged for independence and liberty. Creating a strong, stable democratic government that would protect the rights of its citizens was the formidable job of the framers of the Constitution.

The representative democracy developed by the framers was unique in its structure. In order to guard against an overly strong central government, the United States government would have three separate but equal branches. The executive branch, which included the president and his cabinet, would oversee the administration of the government, approve or disprove legislative actions, enforce the law, command the armed forces and direct relations with foreign governments. The legislature, made up of senators and representatives, would write and enact the laws of the nation. The judiciary, of which the Supreme Court is the highest body, would interpret these laws and make sure that no law enacted by Congress was unconstitutional; that is, that no law violates the essential rights delineated in the Constitution.

In addition, defining and protecting civil liberties was another top priority for the framers. Within the main body of the Constitution are found a number of guarantees of personal freedom and limitations on the authority of government. Among those rights are these:

- There may be no religious test for public office.
- The writ of *habeas corpus* may not be suspended. (Habeas corpus guarantees that a person cannot be kept in prison indefinitely without being appropriately charged with a crime.)
- *Ex post facto* laws may not be passed. (These are laws that make an individual liable for an act that was not a crime before the law was passed.)

- Bills of attainder may not be passed. (A bill of attainder punishes without a trial. For example, a law ordering all blue-eyed people to prison would be a bill of attainder.)
- Titles of nobility are prohibited.

In view of these limitations on the power of the government, many framers of the Constitution felt the main body of the document provided the people with adequate protection. For example, if Congress had been given no power to meddle with religion, was it then necessary to make a further statement about it? Moreover, was it possible to make a list of the rights of Americans and would it not be dangerous to make such a list that, by itself, would appear to suggest that Americans have only those rights that are thus enumerated?

On the other hand, despite the safeguards implicit in this system of checks and balances and in these constitutional provisions, citizens of the new United States of America were demanding a Bill of Rights. Without these guarantees, the great American experiment in democracy could not begin.

# CHAPTER TWO

# Making History

The United States Constitution was sent to the 13 new American states for ratification without a Bill of Rights attached. Five states—Connecticut, Pennsylvania, New Jersey, Delaware, and Georgia—signed immediately. Massachusetts approved it by a bare majority, as did Maryland, South Carolina and New Hampshire. But four states were left and at least two—New York and Virginia—were needed for ratification.

Two men, James Madison of Virginia and Alexander Hamilton of New York, led the battle for ratification in those states. They each had very different ideas about the Bill of Rights. Hamilton was firmly opposed, feeling that such a thing as personal liberty could not be legislated. To those who sought additional safeguards in the form of a Bill of Rights, he asked, "Why declare that things shall not be done which there is no power to do?"

James Madison was one of the preeminent promoters of the Bill of Rights. He felt that we could not trust that the government would not interfere with individual rights: governments were made of people, and history showed how easily people in power abused their authority. The people, for example, could still be whipped and imprisoned for speaking out against the government because they had no such constitutional protections.

Democracy alone, Madison felt, would not be enough to protect the people. In fact, the "tyranny of the majority" could very well overwhelm the minority if the right to speak even the most unpopular views was denied.

In the end, what many of the Founding Fathers had not counted on was the overwhelming demand among the colonists for a Bill of Rights. Since most states had such documents attached to their own constitutions, it should not have been surprising to the Constitution's framers that the people would expect a similar document attached to a national Constitution.

A Bill of Rights had to be promised before the Constitution could be ratified by the nine states required to bring the new government into being. Finally, after two years spent drafting 10 amendments to the new constitution, the Bill of Rights—one of the most remarkable documents in democratic history—was passed into law by the First Congress in 1791.

The first 10 amendments to the United States Constitution are called the Bill of Rights. They are summarized as follows:

Amendment One forbids Congress to enact laws establishing religion or prohibiting the free exercise of religious worship. Moreover, the amendment continues, freedom of speech, press, assembly and petition may not be abridged.

Amendment Two guarantees the right of Americans to bear arms.

Amendment Three prohibits the quartering of soldiers in private homes in peacetime without the owner's consent.

Amendment Four outlaws unreasonable searches and seizures.

Amendment Five is a complex, multifaceted amendment which guarantees prosecution of felonies by indictment, forbids double jeopardy (being tried twice for the same offense) and compulsory self-incrimination (being forced to testify against oneself) and forbids the deprivation of life, liberty or property without due process of law. It also forbids the taking of private property for public use without fair payment.

Amendment Six guarantees a speedy and impartial trial and a local jury in criminal cases.

Amendment Seven provides for jury trial in civil actions.

Amendment Eight prohibits excessive bail, fines and cruel and unusual punishments.

Amendment Nine provides that rights not specifically listed should not be considered denied.

Amendment Ten provides that the powers not expressly delegated to the federal government are reserved to the states and the people.

Today, there are 26 amendments to the Constitution. They range from prohibiting slavery (Amendment Thirteen) to granting women the right to vote (Amendment Nineteen) to prohibiting the payment of a tax as a qualification for voting (Amendment Twenty-four). Amendment Fifteen sought to give the vote to former slaves. One of the most complex and important is the Fourteenth Amendment, which provides that all persons born or naturalized in the United States are citizens regardless of race or color. No state, the amendment continues, can deprive any person of life, liberty or property without due process of law. The equal protection clause of the Fourteenth Amendment bars any state from denying any person the equal protection of the law.

When the Bill of Rights was adopted, it limited only the power of the federal government. Gradually, but with increasing momentum after 1920, the Supreme Court interpreted the Fourteenth Amendment so that nearly all of the guarantees of the Bill of Rights applied to the states, as well. This was particularly true of the protection afforded the people under the First Amendment.

## Breathing Life into the First Amendment

The First Amendment, which guarantees freedom of expression, is the main concern of this book. While the other amendments provide mainly procedural safeguards against unfair trials, arbitrary arrests and harsh punishments, the First Amendment deals with the substantive rights without which democracy would be impossible. These freedoms of speech, press, petition and assembly, however, are but bony skeletons that must be given the breath of life. The Supreme Court of the United States bears the greatest responsibility for doing so.

The Constitution is the supreme law of the land, but as former Chief Justice Charles Evans Hughes declared, "the Constitution is what the Supreme Court says it is." Through its interpretation of federal and state laws, the Court tells us the extent and the limits of freedom of expression. Former Justice Hugo Black described this function well when he wrote in *Chambers v. Florida* (1940), a case involving issues of a fair trial, "Under our constitutional system, courts stand against any winds that blow as havens of refuge for those who might otherwise suffer because they are helpless, weak, outnumbered ...."

With its nine members, who are appointed for life, the Supreme Court is the highest court in the land. It has been called "America's unique contribution to the theory of government." The Supreme Court deals with two kinds of cases: It has original jurisdiction (it hears them first) in cases affecting ambassadors and other public ministers and in those cases to which a state is a party; and it handles appeals from those parties who have not found redress in the lower courts.

Its most famous cases, however, involve questions of the constitutionality of federal and state laws. These cases have to do with whether or not a law, enacted by the Congress or a local government, is in conflict with the Constitution.

The importance of the Supreme Court is not only that there is no further appeal from its decisions but also that its decisions are binding upon similar cases throughout the nation. On the other hand, the Supreme Court has no independent powers of law enforcement and so depends on the states and the national government to enforce its decisions.

Often, the enforcement of controversial Supreme Court decisions is difficult to achieve. In May, 1954, for example, when the Supreme Court of the United States declared segregated public schools unconstitutional (*Brown v. Board of Education of Topeka*), the court urged that segregation be ended "with all deliberate speed." But in the North as well as in the South, there was a good deal of sometimes violent opposition to desegregation. Even today, segregation remains a shameful problem in many school districts throughout the country.

Because it lacks its own enforcement apparatus, the power of the Supreme Court is largely moral in character. The people look to the Court as the ultimate guardian of their rights. Because of the esteem in which the Court is held by the people, the president, Congress and the states generally accept and carry out its decisions.

Nevertheless, it is the people and not the Court that must be the first guardian of their own liberties. In other words, the Court is not empowered to render decisions unless the people, through the lower courts, first initiate legal procedures against what they perceive to be infringements of their liberties.

There is no automatic review of the laws of Congress or acts of state legislatures. Legislation from these bodies often does infringe on the ability of the people to express themselves freely, yet the Supreme Court can do nothing about such transgressions unless "we, the people" get so overwrought as to be willing to take the time, expend the energy and spend the money to achieve redress of our grievances through often painstaking legal means.

Nor is the Supreme Court obligated to hear every case that comes to it upon appeal. Quite the contrary—the Court can pick and choose those cases it wishes to hear. It is difficult to assess why the Court chooses to review some cases and refuses to review others, but the nature, timing and potential impact of the case all go into determining which cases the Court will accept and which it will not.

A decision of the Supreme Court is made by majority vote. Often the vote is very close, as in the many 5 to 4 decisions that win by just one vote. Majority and minority opinions are written by one or more members on each side. The minority or dissenting view discusses why the justices disagree with the decision of the majority and often paves the way for new thinking and further refinement of legal precedents; the minority opinion of one generation often becomes the majority view of the next. The dissents of such eminent jurists as Harlan, Holmes, Brandeis, Black and Douglas became the conscience of the country and prepared the way in many cases for later majorities.

Sometimes it is said that the Court "follows the election returns." That is, the majority decisions of the Supreme Court reflect the way people are voting on the issue at the time. To some degree this is true. But it is also true that the Court is often at the cutting edge of controversial issues, forcing people to walk paths they have feared to tread. On such issues as school desegregation and abortion, the Court ventured opinions that remain highly controversial today.

In the area of freedom of expression, the Court's main function is to determine limits. The people want to express their views freely, orally and in writing, silently and symbolically. The government, on the other hand, wants to limit such expression in the interests of what it perceives to be the common good. A classic example may be found in the prerogatives of wartime: In the interests of what it believes to be necessary to win a war, the government may impose barriers to freedom of expression. But the Court must decide whether freedom of expression in a particular case does, indeed, pose a danger to the war effort. As a matter of fact, the views the government may find objectionable may be just those views that enable it to achieve peace sooner. To silence their expression may in this way delay the war's end.

When does one person's freedom of expression impair the freedom of another to express opposing views? Rights often conflict, and in such cases the United States Supreme Court is called on to decide. On other occasions, the issue is not freedom of expression itself but how that freedom is exercised. The demonstrations of students in the 1960s on college campuses are a case in point. Did the students have the right to express themselves by sitting in on the office of a college president or by burning a research facility (University of Wisconsin) or an auditorium (the College of the City of New

York)? How should men and women today who oppose the Bush administration's activities in Latin America behave? Do parents have the right to insist on labels on record albums, or does that breach the artists' right of free speech? Can animal rights activists interfere with customers who wish to buy a fur coat? These are among the conflicting issues the United States Supreme Court is called on or may be called on to decide.

In the past, a number of limits to free speech have been drawn—by society, by the government and by the Supreme Court. Some of the most commonly cited limits to free speech in the United States follow.

**Free Speech and National Security**

Balancing the right to dissent with the government's need for security and domestic unity has been a major testing ground for First Amendment rights. Full and open discussion of matters relating to war and defense is, if anything, more vital than any other area to the life of a democracy. On the other hand, military operations, by their very nature, often must be kept secret to be effective. As we'll discuss further in Chapter Three, from the earliest days of our history through the invasion of Grenada in 1985, the tension between these two imperatives has led to many First Amendment fights.

Clearly, there are times when the actions of the military establishment must be protected from the First Amendment right of the people to know about them. We accept that members of the armed forces, for instance, should not be allowed to discuss ongoing military maneuvers if by doing so they could endanger security. The giving or selling of military secrets to foreign governments is also almost universally decried.

On the other hand, there have been a number of laws enacted in the name of national security, and upheld by the Supreme Court, under which civilians have been restricted in what they can say or do against the actions of the United States government.

During World War I, for instance, two laws together known as the Espionage Acts made it a felony "to incite mutiny or insubordination in the ranks of the armed forces" or to "disrupt or discourage recruiting or enlistment service, or utter print or publish disloyal, scurrilous, or abusive language about the form of government, the Constitution, soldiers and sailors, flag or uniform of the armed forces or by word or act support or favor the cause of the German Empire or its allies in the present war, or by word or act oppose the cause of the United States." As we shall see in Chapter Three, the broad language used in this law made it an easy target for a number of different First Amendment fights.

**Shouting Fire and Fighting Words**

Apart from cases of national security directly related to an American war effort, free speech is also restricted in order to keep internal domestic order. Disturbing the peace by shouting on the street at four o'clock in the morning is not an issue of free speech. Deliberately harassing someone, knowing that one's words could cause a riot or a fight, is also against the law.

In the case of *Chaplinsky v. New Hampshire*, for instance, Mr. Chaplinsky shouted, "You are a God-damned racketeer and a damned Fascist, and the whole government of Rochester are Fascists or agents of Fascists" after he was arrested for aggressively distributing leaflets. Chaplinsky was convicted under a law that made it a crime to address any offensive or annoying word to any other person in a public place. The conviction was sustained by the United States Supreme Court, which deemed Mr. Chaplinsky's words to be "fighting words" and hence not a form of speech covered by the First Amendment.

Another concept that has been used to define the limits of free speech is that coined by the eminent Justice Oliver Wendell Holmes in 1919: "The most stringent protection of free speech would not protect a man in falsely shouting fire in a theater and causing a panic." In this instance, Justice Holmes was referring to some leaflets distributed to World War I draftees urging them not to fight. It was the Court's judgment that, because the United States was at war, such comments could (although there was no evidence that they did) cause a panic.

**Obscenity and Pornography**

In 1989, a controversy raged over the work of Robert Mapplethorpe, a photographer who died of AIDS. His photographs were often sexually explicit, and many people considered them to be obscene. The National Endowment for the Arts, a governmental funding institution, was in the process of reconsidering its grant to an art gallery preparing to exhibit Mapplethorpe's work when the gallery itself decided to cancel the show.

Debates have always been conducted in government and private circles over what is appropriate and what is obscene. In the case of Mapplethorpe, the issue was complicated by controversy over what role the U.S. government should have in funding and promoting art that shocks or offends.

During the 1980s, other discussions of obscenity centered on book banning in schools and libraries. Parents wanting to protect their children from literature or textbooks deemed by some as inappropriate brought their message to school boards across the country.

Lewd, obscene or profane words or images are not considered speech under the First Amendment and therefore are not protected by it. However, what is lewd and obscene speech? The matter is complicated and sensitive, and few judicial guidelines have been established in this area. As a result, there are often bitter fights about what is obscene and what is not in novels, plays and other forms of speech.

## Libel and Slander

Also not protected by the First Amendment are slander (attempting to destroy the reputation of another through speech) or libel (attempting to destroy the reputation of another through writing). Together these charges are known as defamation of character. To be considered defamation, the words spoken or written must be proved inaccurate by the person wrongfully defamed and must be heard or read by at least one other person.

In other words, if a newspaper reports that a famous congressman was drunk at a meeting but the congressman can prove that he was sober, the paper has committed the crime of libel and is required to pay damages to the congressman. If, on the other hand, a reporter, in a private conversation with the congressman, accuses him of being drunk, no charge of libel or slander could be made.

## The Right to a Fair Trial

The Sixth Amendment to the Constitution states that "in all criminal prosecutions, the accused shall enjoy the right to a speedy and public trial, by an impartial jury . . . ." This right to a fair trial often conflicts with the right of the public to know and the right of the press to report, and a balance must be struck between the two. An excess of "free speech" before a trial, as when a community is flooded with press or TV coverage of a crime, can make it impossible for an impartial jury to be chosen. During a trial, both prosecutors and defense attorneys have been known to "try their cases in the media," therefore exerting pressure on judges and juries to return verdicts expected by the "overinformed" public.

When such basic rights as free speech and a fair trial conflict, how do we decide which is more important? Is freedom of speech—the bedrock of our democracy—*always* more important than other societal needs?

## The Preferred Position of the First Amendment

It is often inviting for the Supreme Court to limit freedom of speech when the speech is of a kind the overwhelming majority of Americans deplore. The Court tries to avoid this temptation lest it find itself on the slippery slope that leads to the imposition of excessive restraints.

The First Amendment is the great affirmative promise of the Bill of Rights and traditionally has enjoyed a "preferred position" in our Constitution. That is, in a conflict between freedom of expression and other values in our society (for example, the value of law and order), the Court has generally given preference to the First Amendment. Chief Justice Harlan F. Stone held that the First Amendment occupied the highest position in the hierarchy of constitutional rights and should be strongly protected against attack in and out of government.

Despite this mandate, however, such protection is not always the case. There are times when both the Supreme Court and society judge that other needs, whether of national security or public standards of morality, are more important. As a result, the preferred position of the First Amendment requires constant nurturing lest the freedoms it protects slowly erode away.

Like a prism of many facets, freedom of speech has come to mean many things. Because "money talks," freedom of expression has been interpreted to include the way in which a candidate for political office raises and spends money for the electoral campaign, and it also includes commercial speech such as the right of professionals, banks and businesses or corporations to engage in some forms of advertising. That real estate agents may post "For Sale" signs on the lawns of homes they are seeking to sell is a right protected by the First Amendment.

The First Amendment protects the rights of women and minorities to press their views and to fight for the removal of discriminatory practices. Those who oppose abortion and those who seek to protect the freedom to choose whether or not to have an abortion are all protected when airing their views vocally, in signs, on television or through meetings and demonstrations.

New issues of free speech are being raised every day. Reporters want to know if nuclear weapons are being stored in a particular town, while the military may want to protect that information. Teachers want to offer their students a certain reading list while the students' parents want to be able to forbid the use of certain texts. Yet, as we've seen, freedom of speech is not absolute; there are limits to what one can say and under what circumstances one can say it. And because these limits change as our society evolves, they are constantly tested, requiring interpretation and revision.

In its deliberations, "the court, like a tree surgeon, has been able to prune off dead and diseased branches [of the Constitution] and to graft on needed new branches." As a result of this pruning process, the United States Constitution remains a living document as pertinent to the 21st century as it was to the 18th century, when it was written.

# CHAPTER THREE

# Issues of National Security

"Were it left to me," wrote Thomas Jefferson in 1787, "to decide whether we should have a government without newspapers, or newspapers without government, I would not hesitate a moment to choose the latter."

Prior to the French Revolution (1789–1799), French society was divided into three groups or "estates." But the press of day played such an important role in the Revolution that it was dubbed the "fourth estate." We use that term to describe the media today because, in addition to the three branches of our government—the executive (president), legislative (Congress) and judicial (courts)—we consider the press and all the media of mass communication to be a fourth, unofficial branch. The media acts as a monitor, checking the effectiveness of the other three.

Those who drafted the First Amendment could have limited themselves to a statement about free speech alone and assumed that it would be understood that the amendment referred to the printed word as well as the spoken. But they chose to be explicit and add freedom of the press as well.

Accordingly, Justice Potter Stewart believed that the Founding Fathers gave the press a special position by singling out "freedom of the press" for special mention. In Stewart's opinion, the news media were "a fourth institution outside the government," serving as "an additional check on the three official branches."

During times of war or domestic turmoil, the role of the "fourth estate" is especially important to a democracy such as ours. It is at such times that many First Amendment challenges have been raised.

## The American Revolution

Even before the Bill of Rights was passed into law in 1791, colonial America already had fought many free speech fights. Perhaps the most famous and important colonial case was that of John Peter Zenger, a New York printer.

In 1733, Zenger became editor of the *New York Weekly Journal* and as editor kept up a steady drumbeat of criticism against William Cosby, the royal governor of New York. In 1734, Zenger was indicted for the crime of seditious libel after printing newspaper articles severely mocking the government of the colony. Seditious libel is material that is written not only to criticize a government but also to stir people to rebellion. During this time, the Crown was particularly sensitive to signs of revolution in its colonies.

Unable to raise bail, Zenger stayed in prison but continued to smuggle out articles to his wife. With the help of friends and financial backers, she kept the newspaper going while her husband was on trial.

Initially, Zenger was defended by James Alexander, a distinguished New York attorney who was the moving force behind the *New York Weekly Journal* and probably the author of some of the articles that so angered Governor Cosby.

Alexander sought to develop the idea that one could not be punished for seditious libel if what is written is true.

When Alexander was debarred in the pretrial stages of the case because he accused the presiding judge of bias, he persuaded Andrew Hamilton of Philadelphia to come to Zenger's defense. It was this "Philadelphia lawyer" who elaborated on the doctrine that truth was the defense against libel. In his summary to the jury, Hamilton declared,

> "As you see, I labor under the weight of many years and am borne down with great infirmities of body; yet old and weak as I am, I should think it my duty if required, to go to the utmost part of the land where my service could be of any use in assisting to quench the flame of prosecutions by the Government to deprive a People of ... arbitrary attempts of men in power .... The question before the court and you, gentlemen of the jury, is not of small or private concern, it is not the cause of a poor printer nor of New York alone which you are now trying: No! It may in its consequence affect every freeman that lives under a British government on the main of America. It is the best cause. It is the cause of liberty ... both of exposing the truth and opposing arbitrary power ... by speaking and writing Truth."[1]

In 1736, Zenger wrote an account of his own trial. He described how the jury withdrew to deliberate his fate, then came back in a short time and, upon being asked by the clerk whether they had agreed on a verdict, responded through its foreman: "Not guilty." When the verdict was rendered the crowd in the courtroom jumped to their feet and cheered, and order was not easily restored. Zenger was discharged from prison. Gouverneur Morris, who as a member of the Constitutional Convention was one of the Founding Fathers, believed Zenger's acquittal represented the "morning star of that liberty which revolutionized America."

## The First Sedition Act

Morris was a little ahead of himself. Censorship in the colonies by one means or another did not die out at once. As would be true throughout our history, when the nation is in crisis, freedom of expression is threatened. An early illustration of this grew out of a power play between the ambitions of France and Great Britain for world domination. John Adams, as second president of the United States, sought to maintain a policy of neutrality for the fledgling nation. However, as relations between France and the United States deteriorated, an undeclared naval war between the two countries ensued.

Because France had helped America during the Revolution, there were many who were critical of the anti-French policy of the Adams administration. To deal with its critics, Congress passed and the president signed the Naturalization, Alien and Sedition Acts of 1798. The Naturalization Act extended the required period of residence for United States citizenship to 14 years. The Alien Act gave the president power to expel foreigners who were conspiring with the enemy. But it is the Sedition Act that most concerns us here.

Under the Sedition Act, seditious libel—speaking or writing against the president or Congress "with the intent to defame"—was still a crime punishable by fine or imprisonment. Taking a lesson from Andrew Hamilton in the Zenger case, however, the law provided that the defense against seditious libel was the truth as presented to a jury in a fair trial. Seditious libel, however, even when the truth is recognized as an acceptable defense, places a severe limit on the meaning of freedom of the press. The need to convince a jury that what the critic has written is indeed the truth is extremely difficult.

The Sedition Act was enforced with a heavy hand. Because justified criticism of government and political opposition were often confused with sedition, the law led to the arrest of 25 men and the conviction of 10, including one member of Congress. In addition, several editors were silenced by heavy fines or jail sentences.

The Sedition Act was never reviewed by the United States Supreme Court. It raised a good deal of resentment against the Federalists, the political party in power at the time, and contributed to the success of their opponents the Republicans (not the present Republican Party) in the presidential election of 1800. Under Thomas Jefferson, who became the third president (1801–1809), the Alien and Sedition Acts were repealed.

## World War I: Freedom of Expression Under Fire

While the Zenger case marks the initial triumph of press freedom in America, no one case and no one victory can assure freedom of the press for all time. It needs to be constantly cultivated and reinterpreted against new challenges, changing technologies and critical times.

One of the most crucial periods in our First Amendment history came during World War I, when the government cracked down on dissent more severely than ever before or since. Thousands of people—from religious pacifists to socialists to labor leaders—were prosecuted for voicing anti-war sentiments at rallies or in writing.

The Espionage Act of 1917 was designed to punish treason in times of war. Under the law, it became a crime punishable by a 20-year jail term to "willfully convey false reports or false statements with intent to interfere with the operation or success of the military or naval force of the United States or to promote the success of its enemies ... or attempt to cause insubordination, disloyalty, mutiny or refusal of duty in the military or naval forces of the United States or ... willfully obstruct the recruiting or enlistment service of the United States."

A year later, an amendment to the Espionage Act, called the Sedition Act, was added. The Sedition Act made it a crime "to utter, print, write or publish any disloyal, profane, scurrilous or abusive language" about the U.S. government or its war efforts.

One of the cases prosecuted under these laws was *Debs v. United States* (1919). Eugene V. Debs, leader of the Socialist Party and many times a candidate for the presidency of the United States, was a pacifist who made a speech opposing the American war effort. "You need to know," he told his audience, "that you're fit for something better than slavery and cannon fodder."[2] The trial judge instructed the jury that they could convict Debs if they believed that the intent of his speech was evil. This broad terminology offered virtually no protection to freedom of expression because "evil" is in the eye of the beholder. Anyone who disagrees with the prevailing view could be considered to have evil intentions.

The jury found Debs guilty of evil intent, and the Supreme Court upheld his conviction. At age 63, Debs began serving a 10-year sentence. While in prison, he ran for the presidency once again and received 919,000 votes. His sentence was commuted by President Harding in 1921.

Five years later, in another case, *Gitlow v. New York* (1925), the Court described the "evil intent" doctrine this way: "That a State in the exercise of its police power may punish those who abuse this freedom of speech by utterances inimical to the public welfare, tending to corrupt public morals, incite to crime, or disturb the peace, is not open to question."

Another important case of the period was *Schenck v. United States* (1919), in which Justice Oliver Wendell Holmes set down his landmark "clear and present danger" test—a test cited by jurists in a variety of cases ever since. Charles

Schenck, general secretary of the Socialist Party of Philadelphia, and Elizabeth Baer, recording secretary, were accused of subverting the war effort by circulating leaflets to draftees urging them not to "submit to intimidation" by fighting a war on behalf of "Wall Street's chosen few." There was nothing in the material that urged draftees to lay down their arms or otherwise take illegal measures to desert, and no evidence was presented that any of the draftees were even influenced by the document. The defendants claimed that their freedom of speech had been denied.

Writing an opinion for a unanimous court, Justice Holmes recognized that the pamphlet did not urge violence to oppose conscription, and he even went so far as to say that under other circumstances the defendants would ordinarily have the right to express their opposition to conscription. "But," commented the Justice, "the character of every act depends upon the circumstances in which it is done." He then upheld the conviction and went on to write what may have become the most often quoted paragraph in Supreme Court history:

> The most stringent protection of free speech would not protect a man in falsely shouting fire in a theater and causing a panic. It does not even protect a man from an injunction against uttering words that may have all the effect of force.

Justice Holmes went on to say that the defendants' pamphlets created "a clear and present danger" of hindering the war effort.

The analogy of shouting fire has been used again and again by those who would seek to limit freedom of expression. Alan M. Dershowitz, a distinguished Harvard professor of law, recently took the eminent Justice Holmes to task for creating a false analogy. The defendants' pamphlets contained a political message, and what they sought was freedom of speech to deliver that message, but shouting fire to create a panic contains no such political message. It urges its hearers to act, not to think. When there is no political message, the analogy of shouting "Fire!" may be appropriate; for example, dialing 911 when there is no emergency, or pretending to pull a gun in the presence of the president, could be considered not acts of free speech but of "shouting fire." But, too often, Holmes's doctrine has been used to limit freedom of speech rather than to enhance it.

In the *Schenck* case, Justice Holmes first alluded to the "clear and present danger" doctrine as a guide for determining the limitation of freedom of speech. However, it was in his famous dissent (concurred in by Justice Brandeis) in *Abrams v. United States* (1919) that the doctrine received greater emphasis.

The defendants in the *Abrams* case were five men and a woman who were indicted under the Sedition Act. As in the *Schenck* case, the defendants had printed leaflets in Yiddish and English denouncing President Woodrow Wilson. The leaflets said, "Workers in the ammunition factories, you are producing bullets, bayonets, cannon to murder not only the Germans, but also your dearest, best, who are in Russia and are fighting for freedom." The leaflets were poorly printed and were distributed by being thrown out of the window of a loft on Houston Street on New York's Lower East Side.

The United States Supreme Court affirmed the conviction of the defendants, insisting that they had "evil intent" inasmuch as the purpose of the leaflets was to inhibit the government's effort to win the war against Germany. It was true that while their purpose may have been evil, the poorly printed documents and the haphazard way in which they were distributed could not possibly have had any adverse influence on the war effort. Nevertheless, the majority of the

Court found the defendants guilty under the second Espionage Act and sentenced them to 20 years imprisonment.

In his notable dissent, however, Justice Holmes went back to the "clear and present danger" principle he had first stated in the *Schenck* case. "In this case," declared the Justice, "sentences of 20 years imprisonment have been imposed for the publishing of two leaflets that I believe the defendants had as much right to publish as the government has to publish the Constitution of the United States now vainly invoked by them."

In the *Schenck* case, Holmes found that "a clear and present danger" to the war effort existed, but he could find no such evidence in the *Abrams* case. In the *Schenck* case, the circulars had been systematically mailed to draftees. In the *Abrams* case, they had merely been thrown out of a window. Holmes said, "Congress certainly cannot forbid all effort to change the mind of the country."

He then went on to apply the analogy of competition in the free economic market to competition in the market of ideas as the "best test of truth." "... we should be eternally vigilant," he continued, "against attempts to check the expression of opinions that we loathe and believe to be fraught with death, unless they so imminently threaten immediate interference with the lawful and pressing purposes of the law that an immediate check is required to save the country." The "silly" leaflet, published by an "unknown man," could hardly hinder the government's war effort.

If the evil intent principle had the effect of inhibiting free speech, the clear and present danger test is considered by civil libertarians as the most useful guideline for expanding free speech.

Some 50 years later, when our nation was again embroiled in war, these tests and others would be applied in new First Amendment cases during the 1960s and 1970s.

## The Vietnam War Period

The Vietnam War was without doubt the most controversial war the United States has fought. For the first time, war was televised—brought into American livingrooms night after night on network news. Hundreds of thousands of young people, and a growing number of their parents, were taking to the streets to protest the war and the government conducting it.

The courts were soon filled with people arrested during demonstrations and charged with burning their draft cards or inciting riots. In 1968, for example, the Supreme Court upheld the conviction of David O'Brien for burning his draft card in Boston. O'Brien, 19 years old, was convicted under a 1965 law that made it illegal to "knowingly destroy" or "knowingly mutilate" a draft card.

Two major cases of the time involved the media. Both newspaper publishers and television editors found themselves in court, fighting for the right to tell the story of the war to a public eager to learn the truth about the nation's longest, most costly war.

### *U.S. v. The Washington Post and the New York Times*

In 1967, at the request of Robert McNamara, then secretary of defense, several highly classified studies of the Vietnam War were gathered. Soon to be known as the Pentagon Papers, they consisted of a series of 47 volumes weighing 60 pounds, containing some 7,000 pages and 2½ million words, of secret government documents that dealt with how the United States came to be involved in the war. Officially known as "History of U.S. Decision-Making Process on Vietnam Policy," the Pentagon Papers were written by a team of distinguished experts and described U.S. involvement in

Vietnam through 1968. Daniel Ellsberg, a former assistant to McNamara, and Anthony Russo, Ellsberg's colleague, now dismayed at our continued involvement in the Vietnam War, "leaked" the document to the *New York Times*.

On June 13, 1971, the *New York Times* began to run a series of articles based on the Pentagon Papers and also printed excerpts from them. The *Washington Post*, which had also obtained the documents, began a similar series of articles and excerpts. Through John Mitchell, then attorney general of the United States, the government immediately sought an injunction to suppress their publication on the grounds that such publication would imperil the security of the United States. For the first time in history, the federal government urged that a document not be published (prior restraint) for fear that what it revealed might adversely affect national security.

The government's attempts to halt publication met with partial success when the courts ruled that the newspapers could not publish any of the material until all the litigation had ended. Thus, the government did succeed in blocking the news for a time and thereby delaying the public's right to know. But, whereas it often takes years for a case to reach the Supreme Court, so important was this case that the Court was ready to review it in less than a week. On June 30, 1971, by a vote of 6 to 3, the high court decided in favor of the newspapers; both the *New York Times* and the *Washington Post* were free to resume publication.

In writing the majority opinion for the Court, Justice Hugo L. Black reminded the government of the history and purpose of the First Amendment. He wrote, "The Government's power to censor the press was abolished so that the press would remain forever free to censure the government." And, he continued, "Secrecy in government is fundamentally anti-democratic, perpetuating bureaucratic errors. Open debate and discussion of public issues are vital to our national health."

In another concurring opinion, Justice Byron R. White did admit that although publication might damage national security, the government had not made a strong enough case to justify prior restraint. But, he wrote, further publication of the Pentagon Papers "does not mean that the law either requires or invites newspapers or others to publish them or that they will be immune from criminal action if they do so." The Justice Department did try to punish the "leakers," Ellsberg and Russo, but it was unsuccessful and did not attempt to test the power of government to punish the newspapers for disclosing "top secret materials."

**The Selling of the Pentagon**

On Tuesday evening, February 23, 1971, the CBS television network presented a documentary entitled "The Selling of the Pentagon." Presented in prime time, the program dealt with the enormous power and vast expenditure of money of the Defense Department to cultivate a favorable image with the American people. The network anticipated that there would be a strong reaction to the program, especially because during the administration of President Richard Nixon, the White House and the news media were often at odds with one another.

What the network did not expect was that the program would become a platform from which the underlying question of whether or not television news was to have the same degree of First Amendment latitude that was traditionally accorded newspapers and magazines would be explored in some depth.

With Roger Mudd as narrator, the program was critical of how the Defense Department manipulated public opinion through its direct contacts with the public, its use of film to create a favorable impression and its handling of the media, that is, press and television. The program was on the air but 14 minutes when the first telephone calls attacking it were received. Roger Mudd was called "an agent of a foreign power." On the other hand, journalists who regularly covered the Pentagon complained that the program had not gone far enough. Congressman R. Edward Herbert, chairman of the House Armed Services Committee and Representative Harley O. Staggers, chairman of the House Committee on Interstate and Foreign Commerce and its Special Subcommittee on Investigations, began a series of investigations about television's use of documentaries to criticize the government.

Congressman Staggers caused subpoenas to be served on CBS demanding the records upon which "The Selling of the Pentagon" was based. CBS was worried about the subpoenas because some of the techniques it used in interviews may have distorted some of the views of those interviewed and sometimes caused erroneous impressions. In the hearings of the Staggers Special Subcommittee on Investigations, the chairman, in his opening remarks, asked, "... are the producers of television news documentary programs engaging in factually false and misleading filming and editing practices ...?"[3]

While CBS furnished a good deal of the material the committee asked for, it did not provide everything. It did not provide "outtakes," or unused film segments, nor did it indicate payments to persons who appeared in the program. In a speech to stockholders, Frank Stanton, CBS president, said that the issue "boils down to one central and vital question: Is this country going to continue to have a free press or is indirect censorship cynically masquerading as a 'federal standard' to be imposed upon it. The issue is as simple as that—and as crucial."[4] Because CBS refused to furnish the outtakes, the Staggers committee eventually held Frank Stanton and CBS in contempt of Congress.

At about the same time, the *New York Times* began publishing the Pentagon Papers. For 36 hours, the government didn't notice, but as the second installment was going to press the administration began to try to have the publication of the Pentagon Papers suppressed. The day after the Supreme Court upheld the right of the newspaper to publish the papers, the full Committee on Interstate and Foreign Commerce recommended to the House of Representatives that CBS be cited for contempt.

After considerable debate in Congress, the contempt citation failed to win a majority of the representatives. The relatively favorable outcome for CBS was a reflection of the concern of Congress for what it would mean to freedom of expression in the United States were it to sustain the subpoena.

## Freedom of Information

After the Pentagon Papers decision and especially during the Reagan administration, there has been some retreat from the gains made in press freedom. When national security conflicts with individual rights, the former appears to be gaining over the latter.

For example, in *Snepp v. U.S.* (1980), the Court upheld a secrecy agreement imposed by the Central Intelligence Agency (CIA) on a former employee who was critical of the CIA despite the fact that no classified information was revealed. Frank Snepp was one of the last Americans to evacuate Saigon when the city fell to the North Vietnamese in 1975. A principal analyst for the CIA in Vietnam, Snepp had grown disillusioned with both the war itself and the agency's role in it. He resigned from the CIA a year later.

Then, in 1977, he wrote *Decent Interval*, a book that outlined and criticized the CIA's role in the war. According to the contract he signed with the agency when he was first hired, he was supposed to submit all material to the agency before publishing. Snepp did not clear his book, claiming that because it contained no classified information, he should not have to subject it to agency scrutiny.

The Supreme Court, which heard his case in 1980, disagreed. "The government," said the Court, "has a compelling interest in protecting both the secrecy and the appearance of confidentiality so essential to the effective operation of our foreign intelligence service." Snepp was forced to forego $140,000 in book royalties, and many feel that the Court's decision has set back the cause of free speech in favor of national security.

### Freedom of Information and the New Technology

A growing problem related to this issue is how to apply the hard-won principles of press freedom to the rapidly developing technology of communication. A good example of this is how to classify the data available through the Freedom of Information Act, passed by Congress in 1966 and significantly amended in 1974. The act was urged by journalists who felt that excessive secrecy in government was preventing them from carrying out their responsibilities as members of the "fourth estate."

If the public has a "right to know," then the government has an obligation to make information about its activities widely available. The Freedom of Information Act is an attempt to open government to greater scrutiny by making records public. Journalists, public interest groups, private individuals and corporations use the Freedom of Information Act to obtain facts about everything from environmental pollution to individual Federal Bureau of Investigation files. According to one report, the government receives about 500,000 requests for information a year.

But what constitutes information? In recent years, much government material is available only through computers. No "hard copy" in the form of a paper record exists. Is information on a computer chip the kind of data covered by the Freedom of Information Act? Should that information be converted to hard copy in the form of a printout?

Moreover, much of the data in computer banks are easily erased. A press of a button or two and a letter from the president of the United States to the head of a foreign government could be lost forever. Is this desirable? Those who drafted the First Amendment could not even imagine the availability of paperless data, let alone how the First Amendment should be applied to it. That such computerized data would become an issue in the 1980s was scarcely considered even by those who wrote the Freedom of Information Act just 20 years earlier.

The conflict between First Amendment values and the values of national security continues. The future of free speech in America depends on the way in which we deal with such cases and how we balance these two equally important imperatives.

In the next chapter, we'll discuss other circumstances in which an individual's rights are in danger of being compromised by freedom of the press: when false statements are made or printed (libel) and when the media make a fair trial, guaranteed by the Sixth Amendment, impossible. In these instances, what is more important to the ideal of democracy: the right of the press or the right of the individual to privacy and dignity?

CHAPTER FOUR

# The Individual against the Press

A free and uninhibited media is, for the most part, the public's most loyal ally in the struggle for true democracy. Uncovering governmental abuses, informing the public of events around the world and presenting issues of importance for public debate are ways that the media contribute to our democratic processes. There are times, however, when overzealous or deliberately misleading media coverage can, in fact, hinder our individual rights.

According to the Bible, "A good name is rather to be chosen than great riches." And in Shakespeare's *Othello* may be found the lines, "Who steals my purse steals trash; ... But he that filches from me my good name ... makes me poor indeed." Laws of libel are designed to protect a person's most precious heritage, namely, a good reputation. However, freedom of expression is also precious and deserves to be diligently protected. Often, in the process of using the courts to protect a person's reputation, freedom of expression may be dangerously eroded.

In a libel case, one sues for either (or both) monetary damages or a retraction of whatever printed statements or pictures allegedly defamed the plaintiff (the one who complains). Such a suit may conflict with a newspaper's preference to write what it wishes without fear of being taken into court. When freedom of expression clashes with the protection of one's good name, where should the line be drawn?

Anyone who has seen the movie *Absence of Malice* knows the pain and suffering that the glare of the media can cause when directed at someone's personal life. In the movie, a reporter is writing a story on the son of a reputed mobster. During her investigation, she uncovers something embarrassing, but relevant, about one of the man's friends. When the newspaper publishes that information, the friend kills herself because of what has been revealed about her.

In this movie, what was printed was, in fact, true. Equally humiliating, but blatantly false stories have also been printed or broadcast about people—famous and not so famous.

What recourse do people have if something false is printed or televised about them? Legally, one can sue the offending media for libel, but the chances of winning are usually slim, especially for the rich and famous. Today's libel laws make a distinction between public figures and private individuals. When the person defamed is famous, he or she must prove that the media acted with malice—that the reporter knew the information was false but decided to print it anyway. Otherwise, the famous person must accept a sometimes careless media as the price to be paid for celebrity.

The private person, on the other hand, has not asked for the media spotlight and cannot command the attention that a celebrity can to refute the charges made by the press. It is far easier for a private person to sue the media for libel: All he or she must show is that the facts presented are false.

Nevertheless, libel law remains a tricky area of First Amendment rights. The cases discussed in this chapter show some of the ways the Supreme Court has regarded the rights of those accused of defaming public and private persons.

## *New York Times v. Sullivan* (1964)

The black community in Montgomery, Alabama, no longer content to be segregated in the back of the bus, vigorously protested segregation through marches, boycotts and sit-ins. Protests continued as blacks sought to integrate lunch counters, railroad and bus terminals, washrooms and water fountains. They wanted the opportunity of trying on clothing in department stores before making a purchase. They risked assault, imprisonment, even death, to fight local regulations that made it difficult and sometimes impossible for blacks to vote.

"Heed Their Rising Voices," was the headline of a full-page advertisement in the *New York Times* of March 29, 1960, which sought to raise money to continue the demonstrations. A New York group called the Committee to Defend Martin Luther King, chaired by Bayard Rustin, placed the ad. It read, in part, "As the whole world knows by now, thousands of Southern negro students are engaged in widespread, non-violent demonstrations in positive affirmation of the right to live in human dignity as guaranteed by the U.S. Constitution and the Bill of Rights." Over 60 well-known public figures signed the advertisement.

The ad described some of the activities in which the students engaged and also the responses of the police, but in the text of the advertisement, a number of errors were made. For example, the ad said that the students had sung "My Country,

'Tis of Thee," but actually they had sung the national anthem. Further, although nine students had been expelled from college by the State Board of Education, it was not for leading demonstrations at the state capitol, as the ad stated, but for demanding service at a Montgomery lunch counter. There were other misstatements, including the fact that while police had been widely in evidence they did not "ring the campus" as the ad stated. Moreover, Martin Luther King had been arrested but four times (not seven) and had not been brutally treated by arresting officers, as the ad seemed to imply.

Although no names were mentioned in the ad, a libel action was brought by L. B. Sullivan, one of the commissioners of the city of Montgomery. A jury in the Circuit Court of Montgomery County awarded Sullivan $500,000, and the award was upheld by the Supreme Court of Alabama. When the suit was brought to the U.S. Supreme Court, it became a landmark case that enormously expanded freedom of expression, especially as it related to cases of libel.

In writing for the majority, Justice William Brennan so eloquently expressed the role of a free press that to this day his words are quoted where freedom of expression is at issue. Perhaps the most memorable passage states, "Thus we consider this case against the background of a profound national commitment to the principle that debate on public issues should be uninhibited, robust and wide-open." In the process of achieving the goal, attacks on government officials may be "sharp," "vehement" and "caustic," and although in such a debate "erroneous statement is inevitable," this is not enough reason to limit the freedom of the press, which needs "breathing room" to survive.

The Court ruled that public officials could recover damages for libel only if they could demonstrate that a false or defamatory statement was made with "actual malice," with "reckless disregard" of whether it was false or not. Three of the justices would have gone even further and given the press full protection against libel, irrespective of proof of malice. The Sedition Act of 1798 was finally declared unconstitutional, and the Court's ruling was hailed by journalists, publishers, lawyers and scholars as a "new charter of liberty." As one leading scholar of civil liberties declared, "It is an occasion for dancing in the streets."[1]

**The Chilling Effect**

As a result of *New York Times v. Sullivan*, "... no country in the world has offered more legal protection for those wishing to speak out frankly and fearlessly."[2] Yet in some ways the Court's decisions in *Sullivan* and in other cases that followed have had an effect that was not intended; that is, there has since been a vast increase in the number of libel cases brought to the American judicial system and heard by the Supreme Court.

One case, *Herbert v. Lando* (1979), the Court ruled that a public figure who files a libel suit should be allowed to inquire into the "state of mind" of the reporter who wrote the offending story. In this case, an army colonel took exception to a documentary aired on the television program "60 Minutes." The Court allowed the colonel to examine the notes and the outtakes of the show, as well as to question the reporters and editors on how and why they made the decisions they did in putting the story together.

In delivering the Court's majority opinion, Justice Byron White stated that in order to prove "actual malice" public figures must be able to get "direct evidence through inquiry into the thoughts, opinions and conclusions of journalists."

To many, the *Herbert* decision was a blow to First Amendment rights. As Nat Hentoff reported in his book, *The First Freedom*, Walter Cronkite said, "The day after the decision was reached, I was listening to our editorial conference at

CBS News in a way I've never listened before. There's a chilling effect right there. And I realized that if those conversations were ever taped and played back in a libel suit, we'd have no defense."[3]

**The Price of Litigation**

Although the case of *Herbert v. Lando* allows the plaintiff to review a reporter's notes or television outtakes—in effect, to probe the journalist's mind for actual malice—it remains difficult for a public person to sue successfully for libel.

In 1985, the libel cases of General William Westmoreland against the CBS broadcasting network and of former Israeli Defense Minister Ariel Sharon against *Time* magazine attracted national attention and illustrated the impact of both the *Sullivan* and *Herbert* decisions. It should be noted that although these cases deal with national security or military issues, they have a direct impact on personal cases as well.

General Westmoreland sued CBS for $120 million for alleging in a 1982 documentary called "The Uncounted Enemy: A Vietnam Deception" that he led a conspiracy to conceal higher enemy troop levels from President Lyndon Johnson and Secretary of Defense Robert McNamara when he was in charge of the conduct of the war in Vietnam. Although there was some evidence that CBS may have been unfair, it became evident that Westmoreland would not be able to prove that CBS had acted with "reckless disregard of the truth," and the general agreed to an out-of-court settlement. Westmoreland had spent $3.5 million but settled for a statement that CBS "never intended to assert" that he was "unpatriotic or disloyal ..." CBS spent $5 million, and although it "won" the case, its credibility and reporting had been tarnished.

Israeli Defense Minister Ariel Sharon fared a little better than General Westmoreland did, but not much. In his $50 million suit against *Time*, Sharon alleged that he had been defamed in a paragraph that said that he had "consciously intended" to encourage a massacre by Christian Phalangists of hundreds of Palestinians living in the Sabra and Shatila refugee settlements. Although an Israeli investigation had come to the conclusion that Sharon may have been indirectly responsible for the massacres, a U.S. jury agreed that the statement in *Time* had gone too far. But a complete victory over *Time* eluded Sharon because he could not prove that *Time*'s reporting had been either malicious or reckless. According to the standard of the *Sullivan* case, it is not enough to prove error. To the extent that fear of making a mistake inhibits "robust debate," error is not sufficient proof of libel. Nevertheless, *Time* too was faced with a shadow over its credibility.

As the cases of Westmoreland and Sharon illustrate, the costs of litigation are so enourmous that even the threat of being brought into court for libel has had a "chilling effect" on newspapers and journals. They may shun the controversial article and the editorial that may bring them into court. Small publishers are especially fearful because extended litigation, even if they win, can be so costly that they may be forced out of business altogether. While hailed as an undeniable victory for a free press, the decision in the *Sullivan* case has resulted in what some journalists have called "the blanding of newspapers."

Does the *Sullivan* case give the media too much protection? Where does one draw the line? In the opinion of Justice White, Sullivan does give the media too much power by making it too difficult for public officials or celebrities who feel libeled to salvage their good names. Moreover, while some financially marginal journals may be threatened by lawsuits, for the most part the media are big business. In many communities, they are monopolies and are better able to finance their defense than the public people who bring them into court.

Wrapped in the First Amendment, the media have become rich and influential. It is not enough for the media to be free; they must be responsible as well. To say, as the *Wall Street Journal* did many years ago, that a newspaper is affected with no public interest may have been appropriate when there were many newspapers, but can it still be true today when monopoly power is the rule rather than the exception in many communities? Where is the line between the freedom of the media to criticize and the right of those who believe their good names have been blemished to obtain redress? Where do we draw the line between a free press and a responsible one?[4]

## Freedom of Speech versus the Sixth Amendment

Another area in which a direct conflict exists between the rights of an individual and the rights of a free press is in the courtroom. Where should the line be drawn between two conflicting and equally important democratic values: the First Amendment right of a free press to comment and criticize and the Sixth Amendment right of a person accused of a crime to a fair trial?

The case of Dr. Sam Sheppard was one of the first, and most famous, of this kind. In 1954, Dr. Sheppard, a prominent, well-respected osteopath, was accused of beating his wife to death. The publicity surrounding the case, even before he went to trial, was enormous. The public was drenched with information about all aspects of the gruesome murder, including quite incriminating evidence against Dr. Sheppard. One newspaper even printed a public opinion poll that showed that an overwhelming majority of townspeople thought Dr. Sheppard was unquestionably guilty.

Dr. Sheppard was convicted by a jury that had been exposed to this publicity. The question he and his attorneys posed in their appeal was whether or not such publicity made it impossible for him to receive a fair trial. Could those jurors have been impartial? Or had their judgment been impaired by the press coverage?

The Supreme Court ruled that he had not, in fact, been given a fair trial. After spending 10 years in jail, Dr. Sheppard was released, and at a new trial, he was found not guilty of murdering his wife.

In the *Sheppard* decision, the Court refused to indict the press for doing, in effect, what it's meant to do: report vigorously on matters of interest to the public. By doing so, the press keeps a check on the police and the judicial system, an important ingredient in a healthy democratic society.

However, in order to protect the rights of the accused, there must be limits to the information made available to the press. The judge in the *Sheppard* case could have limited press access to the courtroom or ordered the attorneys and witnesses not to speak to reporters. He could even have delayed the trial until the publicity died down or ordered the trial to be conducted in another town. Without these restrictions, a person under Dr. Sheppard's circumstances has almost no chance of receiving a fair trial.

The *Sheppard* decision did not limit the press from trying to get at the heart of the story; it did not place restrictions on the activities of reporters. What it did suggest was that the courts have a responsibility to limit attorneys, witnesses and others involved in the case from speaking to reporters about matters that could prejudice the jury. That principle would be upheld in another case some 20 years later.

### *Nebraska Press Association v. Stuart* (1976)

Erwin Charles Simants, an unemployed handyman of limited intelligence, was accused of killing six members of the neighboring Kellie family, including 10-year-old Florence, who was also raped, and James Henry, 66; Audry Marie, 57; Deanna, 7; Daniel, 5; and David, 32, all of whom had rushed to help Florence when she was attacked.

The gruesome killings shocked the rural community of Sutherland, Nebraska, a village not far from the city of North Platte. Simants fled the scene and remained in hiding for 24 hours. However, in response to his father's plea that he turn himself in, Simants returned to the home of his brother-in-law, William Boggs, where he was immediately arrested by a state police officer and the sheriff.

The case grew in notoriety as hordes of journalists from newspapers and television descended on Sutherland. Rumor fed on rumor, and before long Simants was tried and found guilty in the eyes of the public. The police remained silent, or tried to, but the journalists, whose bosses were insisting that they bring back some sensational stories, pressed the sheriff and other law enforcement officials to talk. Many of them did, unwisely.

Judge Ronald Ruff, in whose court the preliminary hearing was to be held, was young and inexperienced. He was also aware that the actual trial would be conducted by Hugh Stuart, a very experienced judge whose opinion of young Ruff was by no means flattering. Judge Ruff wanted to make no mistakes, and the widespread publicity the case generated made him nervous.

Ruff wanted to limit, if not altogether eliminate, the sensationalism surrounding the case. Despite advice to the contrary, including advice from Judge Stuart, Judge Ruff imposed a "gag" order on what the press could report. The gag order was contrary to the voluntary Nebraska guidelines governing what and how the press could report at a pretrial hearing. What Judge Ruff said at the time appears pertinent: "... the right of the free press must be subservient to the right of the accused to have due process."

While the local press continued to obey the gag order, they chafed under its limitations. Although Judge Stuart had advised against a gag order of any kind, he reversed himself when the case reached his court and drew up what he thought was a narrower one. The judge ordered that the press not publish any confession by Simants, the pathologist's report or the names of those who had been sexually assaulted by Simants.

As the case moved along to trial, the press took increasing offense at the gag orders and maneuvered to persuade the Supreme Court to overturn it. On December 12, 1975, the Court agreed to take the case. On January 7, 1976, Simants was found guilty and 12 days later was sentenced to death in the electric chair.

On June 30, 1976, the gag order was unanimously overturned by the Supreme Court. Chief Justice Burger wrote for the Court, declaring that "the problems presented by this case are almost as old as the republic ... [however] pretrial publicity—even persuasive, adverse publicity—does not inevitably lead to an unfair trial." The Chief Justice cited the *Near* case (see Chapter Five) and the Pentagon Papers case and wrote that "the thread running through all these cases is that prior restraints on speech and publication are the most serious and least tolerable infringement on First Amendment Rights ... We reaffirm that the guarantees of freedom of expression are not an absolute prohibition under all circumstances, but the barriers to prior restraint remain high and presumption against its use continues intact."

In an unusual twist of fate, Simants, who was entitled to an automatic appeal because he was sentenced to death, was found by the Supreme Court of Nebraska to have been denied a fair trial after all. The problem, it turned out, was not the publicity but the fact that the sheriff had visited the jurors three times while they were deliberating the case in a motel. At a new trial, Simants was found not guilty by reason of insanity and is today a patient in a Nebraska mental institution.

First Amendment rights may also conflict with a fair trial when a reporter gathers information that actually is material evidence in the trial. Such a case led to the 1978 conviction of Myron Farber, a *New York Times* reporter, for contempt of court when he refused to name his sources or turn over his notes to the court.

Mr. Farber had done some hard-nosed investigation into a series of deaths that had taken place in a New Jersey hospital some 10 years before. Farber interviewed the staff and the victims' families, examined medical records and talked to other doctors. As a result of Farber's investigation, bodies of victims were exhumed and autopsies conducted. It was discovered that a poison, curare, had been injected into the patients, causing their deaths. After further investigation, a doctor, Mario Jascalevich, was charged with murder.

During Dr. Jascalevich's trial, his attorney demanded that the notes Farber had made during his investigation be turned over to the defense. Because they could prove crucial to the accused's defense, the attorney reasoned, the court should have access to them.

Myron Farber refused, citing a New Jersey statute that protects a reporter from having to reveal his sources. He was cited for contempt and spent nearly six weeks in jail. The *New York Times* paid $285,000 in fines.

In the end, Dr. Jascalevich was acquitted on all counts. When the case was over, Farber was released and the fines for contempt were suspended. But the fundamental First Amendment issue the case raised was never resolved. As the *New York Times* wrote on November 9, 1978, "So while the murder case is over, the case of constitutional rights—and needs—of the press has been left in disarray. ... The notes were refused, even for private inspection by the judge, because we contend that the Constitution's First Amendment, guaranteeing freedom of the press, implies the right of reporters to protect the confidentiality of their source. We maintain that a right to print the news carries with it a right to gather news and that without confidentiality, the sources of much valuable information would dry up."

The protection of an individual's liberties is the main objective of the Bill of Rights. Every time the press, working under the broad boundaries of the First Amendment, interferes with the right of an individual to privacy or to a fair trial, the scales are tipped. It is up to a vigilant public and an even-handed judicial system to balance the scales of justice once again.

CHAPTER FIVE

# Freedom for the Speech We Hate

"The right to free speech is always tested at the extremes," said Aryeh Neier, executive director of the American Civil Liberties Union in April 1978. "Rarely are centrist groups denied their First Amendment rights. It is almost always fringe groups, people who are proactive ... . For that very reason, it is the extremes that have the greatest interest in protecting the rights of their enemies."

Mr. Neier, speaking at a debate over the American Nazi Party's right to march through a Jewish community, sums up an essential concept of our American ideal of free speech. In the words of Justice Oliver Wendell Holmes, "If there is any principle of the Constitution that more imperatively calls for attachment than any other it is the principle of free thought—not free thought for those who agree with us, but freedom for the thought we hate."

In a number of cases, the Supreme Court has had to judge whether the First Amendment applies to subject matter, from racism to pornography, that the majority of Americans find abhorrent.

## *Near v. Minnesota*

After many years and much discussion about prior restraint as an enemy of freedom of expression, it was not until 1931 that the Supreme Court had an opportunity to rule on it. Jay M. Near and his colleague, Howard Guilford, owned the *Saturday Press*, a newspaper in Minneapolis, Minnesota, which specialized in giving offense to its readers. It was anti-Catholic as well as anti-Jewish in its outlook. It blamed crime and corruption in Minneapolis on "Jewish gangsters," as the following sample of its reportorial style amply demonstrates.

"Practically every vendor of vile hooch, every owner of a moonshine still, every snake-faced gangster and embryonic-yegg in the Twin Cities is a Jew. ... I simply state a fact when I say that ninety percent of the crimes committed against society in this city are committed by Jew gangsters. ... It is Jew, Jew, Jew, as long as one cares to comb over the records ... ."[1]

In 1925, a Minnesota law authorized the government to close down by a court order, called an injunction, any "malicious, scandalous and defamatory newspaper, magazine or other periodical" as a "public nuisance." After the newspaper had published a number of articles, all of which hammered away at the theme of Jewish involvement in gangsterism and corruption, the county attorney obtained an injunction prohibiting any further publication of the *Saturday Press*. Specifically, the order of the trial judge prohibited Near and his associates "from producing, editing, publishing, circulating, having in their possession, selling or giving away any publication whatsoever, which is a malicious, scandalous or defamatory newspaper."

Near appealed to the Minnesota Supreme Court, saying that his First Amendment right to freedom of the press had been violated. The state Supreme Court rejected his argument, contending that Near could continue to publish so long as his articles were no longer a "public nuisance." But Near was not satisfied. Where would the line be drawn between what was permissible and what was not, he wondered, and who would draw it? He held that under the guidelines of the state Supreme Court, he risked jail no matter what he published. Mr. Near took his argument to the Supreme Court.

In a 5-4 vote, the Supreme Court held for Near, with Chief Justice Charles Evans Hughes writing the majority opinion. First of all, Hughes cited the history of the First Amendment, which in effect prohibited almost all forms of prior restraint. Near could not be punished in advance for what he wrote; those who were defamed by him could only sue for damages afterward.

In reaching this decision, the Court fell back on an important principle of freedom of expression, namely, that "the rights of the best men are secure only as the rights of the vilest and most abhorrent are protected." If one were to look into the backgrounds of those whose names are on Supreme Court cases, one would find that many of those protected by the Court were people of less than exemplary character. Nevertheless, by protecting them, the rights of men and women of exemplary character are often likewise safeguarded.

The decision of the Supreme Court in the *Near* case was one of the most important in the annals of freedom of expression. If Near's newspaper, however vile, could have been crushed, so could nearly all criticism of public officials. Had Near not prevailed, offended officials who wanted to suppress criticism would need only find a judge who shared their view that the criticism went beyond legitimate bounds.

## The Marketplace of Hate

A question is raised by the *Near* case—should we protect the speech of those who hate or those who would deny essential rights to others? Blacks, who have made highly effective use of the First Amendment to overcome racial discrimination and harassment, often face an interesting free speech dilemma. First Amendment protection made the Freedom Marches and Freedom Rides possible, but in order to overcome continued racial harassment in the form of speech that vilifies their race, is it now justified to place restrictions on that amendment? Said one black activist on the campus of Stanford University, "We don't put as many restrictions on freedom of speech as we should."[2] But should such restrictions be imposed? Is outlawing of racist speech consistent with the guarantees of the First Amendment?

Those who believe that racial slurs and group defamation can be made illegal without doing violence to the First Amendment insist that there is a precedent for their position. They point out that obscenity is not protected by the First Amendment, and what is more obscene than racial epithets accompanied by four-letter words? "Fighting words," which may incite violence, are also prohibited. What is more likely to cause public mayhem than vicious racial slurs?

Furthermore, other democratic societies, like Britain, France, Canada and Sweden, already have laws that prohibit racial slurs that incite violence, yet they are able to remain free, open societies. Those who hold the view that racial slurs should be restricted believe that a line can be drawn that would clearly identify hateful speech without fear of creating a slippery slope that would lead to First Amendment restrictions in other areas.

Those who feel that such restrictions would inevitably lead to further erosion of the First Amendment hold that the answer to offensive speech is more speech, not less. They insist that, in practical terms, any limitation on freedom of speech poses a grave danger to a democratic society. Rather than endanger the expression of unorthodox and minority views, it may be better to allow all who wish to speak to do so. Justice Oliver Wendell Holmes put it elegantly when he said that the most essential constitutional protection is "not free thought for those who agree with us, but freedom for the thought we hate."

With an increase in racial tension in the 1980s and an uncertainty about exactly how to diminish these tensions, the issue of freedom for the speech we hate has become especially sensitive.

"Bleacher creatures" in the stadium of the Detroit Tigers took to calling chants against players who erred and umpires who made bad calls. The chants substituted obscene four-letter words for the beer commercial, "Tastes great! Less filling." Those who heard the obscene chants, including those who could hear it over radio broadcasts, objected.

To accommodate those offended, the Tigers' management put up a sign that said, "No chanting." The American Civil Liberties Union of Michigan, however, insisted that the chanting was a right protected by the First Amendment. The Tigers amended the sign to read "No obscene chanting." The ACLU objected again, insisting that "obscene" lacks clear definition and does not tell the chanter exactly what he or she cannot shout. In this clash of values, whose views should prevail?

On one college campus, a speaker suggested that gay men were far more likely to commit an assortment of heinous crimes than others. Should such a speaker be allowed to "speak his mind" even though what he said insults a group of students?

On another campus, those who opposed apartheid in the Union of South Africa closed down the college library in protest. Should students not so opposed be denied the use of the building?

Flag burning and the burning of crosses are both forms of expression protected by the First Amendment. The first is an expression of hate for America, the latter an expression of hate for blacks. Because both are forms of expression that most Americans loathe, should they be made illegal, even if it means limiting First Amendment protection?

### The Battle of Skokie

The case of the *Village of Skokie v. National Socialist Party of America* (1978) represented one of the most severe tests of the First Amendment. The question had to do with the right of American Nazis, described by one of their own publications as a group of "dead-beats, regalia freaks, right-wing kooks, religious nuts," to stage a rally in Skokie, Illinois.

The Anti-Defamation League, a Jewish group that protects Jewish interests and fights anti-Semitism, concurred that the American Nazis were an essentially impotent group. They did concede, however, that the Nazis were troublemaking rowdies capable of stirring vicious hate propaganda and occasional street violence.

At the time, the American Nazi party was led by George Lincoln Rockwell and included in its membership one Frank Collin, who ironically was a son of Max Cohen, a Jewish concentration camp survivor. Rockwell ousted Collin because of his Jewish roots and Collin formed a Nazi splinter group called the National Socialist Party of America, which despite its pompous name, never consisted of more than two dozen or so people. Collin had a talent for securing widespread media attention for his small group and it was in pursuit of such publicity that he decided, in 1976, to stage a demonstration in Marquette Park in Chicago. That city, however, insisted that the Nazis buy $350,000 worth of insurance in the event of violence. Since the premium on a policy of this size was well beyond his means, Collin sought the assistance of the American Civil Liberties Union (ACLU).

The ACLU filed a suit in Collin's behalf in U.S. District Court alleging restriction on Collin's right to freedom of speech and assembly. In early 1977, while waiting for the case to be heard, Collin sought to sustain the momentum of media attention by writing to ten communities asking permission to demonstrate in their parks. All the communities, with the exception of Skokie, either ignored Collin's letter or wrote vague responses.

The suburban village of Skokie, outside of Chicago, is a small community in which live many Jewish survivors of the Nazi Holocaust. It was not surprising, therefore, that even getting a letter from an American Nazi group proposing a demonstration would provoke anxiety and trigger an immediate outcry. Taking a cue from Chicago, Skokie park officials informed Collin that his group also would have to post a $350,000 bond.

Because Collin could not pay the premium, he announced that he and his associates would hold a quiet demonstration in front of the Skokie Village Hall in protest of the insurance requirement. He insisted that while his demonstrators would be in full Nazi uniform, including the swastika, and would carry signs saying, "Free Speech for White People," there would be no speeches and no distribution of literature. Collin insisted that he was within his right to assemble peaceably as provided in the First Amendment.

The village of Skokie could do one of two things: It could allow the demonstration to go forward, or it could go to court and through an injunction put a halt to the demonstration. The village council decided that to allow the protest would be the lesser of two evils. However, this decision aroused cries of outrage from Holocaust survivors. To one survivor, the protest was not about "freedom of speech but about death." With such irresistible pressure, the Skokie village council reversed itself and decided to try to get an injunction to prohibit the demonstration altogether. Once again, Collin's Nazis sought the help of the American Civil Liberties Union.

A year and a half of legal maneuvers in which the First Amendment was tested followed. But the human spectacle of Jewish attorneys from the ACLU, some of whom were themselves children of survivors of the Holocaust, defending Nazis stirred national interest, aroused passion and riveted American attention on the otherwise quite ordinary community of Skokie. The attorneys for the Nazis were vilified and their lives were threatened. There were many who could not or would not understand the preferred position of the First Amendment and the protection it offers to the thought, to the words and to the right to assemble and petition of those we hate.

In its effort to keep Collin's Nazis from marching on the village, the authorities of Skokie adopted a number of ordinances that have an interest for the issue of freedom of assembly. These ordinances were as follows:

Ordinance 994 required demonstrators to secure a permit at least 30 days in advance and post $350,000 worth of insurance. Permits would be issued only if the village manager found that the activity would not portray criminality, depravity or lack of virtue or incite violence, hatred or abuse of any race or religion.

Ordinance 995 made it a crime to distribute material that incites racial or religious hatred.

Ordinance 996 prohibited marching or demonstrating while wearing a military-style uniform.

Despite these ordinances, Collin, with the help of the ACLU, persisted in demanding his right to demonstrate.

After a number of legal moves and countermoves, the United States Court of Appeals for the Seventh Circuit ruled that the demonstration could be held. In his decision of October 16, 1978, Judge Bernard Decker ruled that the Skokie ordinances were unconstitutional. The insurance requirement was so outrageous as to pose an impossible barrier to the exercise of First Amendment rights and constituted an "abridgement in the guise of regulation." The remaining ordinances were overly broad and were unconstitutional because they were an illegal prior restraint on free speech.

"Freedom of thought," Judge Decker wrote, "carries with it the freedom to speak and to publicly assemble to express one's thoughts. ... it is better to allow those who preach racial hate to expend their venom in rhetoric rather than to be panicked into embarking on a dangerous course of permitting the government to decide what its citizens must say and hear." The United States Supreme Court refused to hear the case on appeal and so, in effect, Collin had won.

The Nazis marched, but not in Skokie. Although he was free to do so, Collin now was free to demonstrate in Chicago as well. Two demonstrations were held, one in Federal Plaza and the other in Marquette Park, as had been originally planned over a year and a half before. A pathetic band of Nazis were protected by Chicago's police, and the debris was cleaned up by Chicago's sanitation workers. The cost to the city of Chicago was in excess of $100,000 without counting legal costs.

Protecting freedom of speech and assembly has its price, but is it just to allow those who would if they could deny fundamental rights to others to wrap themselves in the First Amendment?

The legal "battle of Skokie" highlighted an age-old dilemma. Does the First Amendment protect those who would, if in power, deny its protection to others? The Court has held that it does. Does "vicious" speech deserve the same protection of the First Amendment as does "good" speech? Generally, the court has held that it does, although as in the *Chaplinsky* case (see Chapter One), words that tend to incite, "fighting words," are not served by the First Amendment.

But it is often difficult to judge which words are beyond the scope of the First Amendment. How can one distinguish between "good" and "vicious" speech? If the latter is not protected, how safe is the former? Finally, how important is it to defend the procedure by which the First Amendment is protected when it allows "bad" people to speak and assemble? Here again, because one cannot readily determine who is good and who is bad, the preferred position of the First Amendment suggests that, except in rare cases and only under extreme circumstances, such as when the national security may be threatened, the delicate balance should weigh in favor of rigorous debate.

## Censorship: Protecting Public Morals

The value of freedom of expression often clashes with those who take it upon themselves to protect America's morals by monitoring what people read in books and plays or see in the movies or on television. With the elimination of licensing, censorship in the form of prior restraint was abandoned in colonial America. With the Zenger case, truth was established as a defense against seditious libel. Moreover, the Supreme Court has generally drawn the line loosely around the First Amendment so as to give maximum protection to the value of freedom of speech and freedom of the press. As a result, those who see it as their role to protect the morals of

Americans try to get around the First Amendment and the Court and attempt to curb indirectly what Americans may see or read. Among the more important ways in which they have tried to do so are prohibitions on what could be sent through the mails and what could be received from overseas.

Anthony Comstock, a moral crusader, secured Federal postal legislation in 1873 that prohibited immoral materials from being sent through the mail. At the time, the Supreme Court held that the right of Congress to establish post offices carried with it the right to determine what the post office will exclude. But in 1946, the issue before the Court was still the use of the mail; this time, it was the privilege of sending materials at second-class (lower) postage rates.

Second-class postage was introduced as a way of disseminating "information of a public character, or devoted to literature, the sciences, arts or some special industry." U.S. Postmaster General Hannegan decided that the magazine *Esquire*, the *Playboy* of its day, did not in his view contribute to American morals, and he suspended second-class mailing privileges for the magazine. In *Hanegan v. Esquire* (1946), the Supreme Court set aside the postmaster's action. The Court insisted that what is good literature or good art varies from generation to generation and may be different for each individual. No government can determine for its citizens an official "norm" of "acceptable culture." The requirements of the statute could best be served by uncensored distribution of literature.

Without an official norm of acceptable literary or artistic expression, local communities often took it upon themselves to impose criteria they felt would safeguard the morals of their citizens. Which criteria would best serve this purpose? One possibility was the Hicklin test, which was established in Victorian England and held that a book could be judged on the basis of selected passages rather than as a whole. If a work was judged, for example, to have sexually explicit passages that might be read by the immature or by children, the work as a whole could be declared obscene and banned. This standard meant that an entire book could be suppressed based on a few paragraphs.

Local communities in America at various times have banned the works of authors of international renown such as Rabelais, Shaw, Hardy and Wilde. Theodore Dreiser's *An American Dream,* Sinclair Lewis's *Elmer Gantry,* Lillian Smith's *Strange Fruit* and James T. Farrell's *Studs Lonigan* were among the American books and writers who were banned at different times and places. Sometimes such books were burned and their authors threatened.

Through the control of the Customs Service, the federal government has likewise sought to control the introduction of material from abroad it considered obscene. D. H. Lawrence's *Lady Chatterly's Lover,* Henry Miller's *Tropic of Cancer* and James Joyce's *Ulysses* were among the works deemed by customs to be obscene and barred from entry. Many of these works were widely smuggled past not overly zealous customs officials, but for a considerable period of time they could not be imported legally.

Acting according to their interpretation of the 1890 Tariff Act, U.S. government customs inspectors seized James Joyce's *Ulysses* because they believed it to be obscene. In 1933, in a federal district court in the case of *United States v. One Book Called "Ulysses,"* Judge John Woolsey dismissed a libel suit against the book. In his thoughtful opinion Judge Woolsey asked, "When a real artist in words, as Joyce undoubtedly is, seeks to draw a true picture of the lower middle class in a European city, ought it to be impossible for the American public legally to see that picture?" He ruled that Americans were entitled to read and own *Ulysses* and that a work must be judged as a whole, not merely on the basis of isolated passages. While the decision struck a blow at the Hicklin test, it did not change American censorship patterns at once. It did, however, mark a turning point in that the Court tended to narrow scope of speech that would be considered obscene and so not protected by the First Amendment.

**In the Eye of the Beholder**

The role of censorship in the United States centers on the many times the Supreme Court has tried to define obscenity. Looking back over the Court's history, Chief Justice Earl Warren described the Court's effort to deal with obscenity as its "most difficult" area of adjudication. The following cases will illustrate some of the difficulties.

In 1957, in *Roth v. United States*, the Court explicitly overturned the Hicklin standard of obscenity. To be judged obscene, materials must offend "the common conscience of the community by present day standards." Moreover, the materials must be judged to be "utterly without redeeming social importance." However, Justice Black would later say that such a test was about "as clear as the composition of the Milky Way."

In the case of *Miller v. California* (1973), an attempt was made to establish criteria by which obscenity could be determined. Drawing on *Roth v. United States*, the Court held that to be obscene the material must be taken as a whole. Merely the inclusion of selected titillating passages is not enough to condemn a work. Moreover, the work as a whole must clearly appeal to the "prurient interest." That is, its sole purpose must be to arouse sexual desire. There must be evidence that the work contains offensive descriptions of sexual behavior and it must be clearly evident that the work is without any redeeming features of literary, artistic, political or scientific value (LAPS). LAPS became a sort of "obscenity yardstick" by which local communities could determine for themselves whether these criteria were applicable to offensive material and how they ought to be applied.

As ill-defined as obscenity is, indecency is even more elusive of definition. While the former is not protected by the First Amendment the latter is; the distinction is often obscure to say the least. The Court held only that indecency is that which a community finds "patently offensive." It is left to "the eye of the beholder" in local communities to identify what is obscene and what is indecent.

### Pornography

"Hard-core" pornography is not protected by the First Amendment. Although this is a term that has been used by the Supreme Court, what does it mean? So difficult is it to define with enough precision so that a line can be drawn between what is protected speech and what is not that Justice Potter Stewart in 1964 threw up his judicial hands and declared, "I know it when I see it." Justice John Harlan was equally dismayed by the difficulty of definition and declared, "One man's vulgarity is another man's lyric." And Harvard's distinguished law professor, Alan Dershowitz, in 1986 expressed the view that because there is no precise definition of pornography, it is impossible to deny it constitutional protection. To do so would be to embark on that ever-present "slippery slope" of endangering freedom of expression altogether.

Public morality and freedom of expression often clash with one another. Those who place an absolute value on the First Amendment hold that public morality is best served when those who wish to dance topless in a bar and those who wish to watch are free to do so. From a wide diversity of materials, the public itself must have the opportunity to choose what they wish to see and read. According to this view, over a period of time, not only is democracy strengthened but the public is more rather than less likely to scorn the pornographic.

There are others who are not so confident in the wisdom of the people to shun pornography, especially when such materials are aggressively thrust at them. This group believes that public morality is best safeguarded when pornography and lewd behavior are banned or at least carefully regulated, even if that means curbing the First Amendment's command that "Congress shall make no law ... abridging freedom of speech or of the press." This group believes that pornography debases men and women. To the extent that a democracy depends on men and women of good character, wildly proliferating pornographic materials put democracy itself at risk. "The more debased the subjects, the safer is the tyrant's rule."[3]

In the eyes of the women's rights movement, pornography is not only about freedom of expression. Instead it is another blatant example of how men try to keep women "in their place"—not merely on matters of sexuality but in the workplace as well. Susan Brownmiller, who wrote *Against Our Will,* believes that pornography is anti-female propaganda similar to racism or anti-Semitism. She believes pornography "... to be a clear and present danger to women and to the health of our society . ..."[4]

An important part of the problem is that no one is quite sure what the effect of pornography is on the people of a nation. In ancient Rome, the populace was entertained by throwing Christians to the lions or by forcing gladiators to fight one another until one or both were mutilated or killed. Violent chariot races likewise stimulated the crowds to frenzy. There are some who feel that such depraved forms of entertainment explain, to an important degree, why Rome fell.

That pornography automatically leads to depravity and fascism is not at all clear. In 1968, a Federal Commission on Obscenity and Pornography appointed by President Lyndon Johnson worked for two years and recommended the end of all restrictions for adults who wish to read sexually explicit books and magazines or look at lewd films and pictures. Twenty years later, another Presidential Commission on Pornography appointed by President Reagan reported that pornography led to violence, that it should be restricted by the federal government, and that the government could do so without violating the First Amendment. In drawing the line on issues of pornography, the Supreme Court is, as always, called on to decide. It is not eager to do so and, as we have seen, waffles on the issue.

In 1989, in the case of *Sable Communications v. FCC*, a unanimous Supreme Court declared that a federal ban on commercial telephone messages that are "indecent" but not "obscene" violates the constitutional right to freedom of expression. While the Court held that Congress could strive to prevent children from hearing sexually explicit messages, it could not shut down the entire industry to do so. "It is another case of burning up the house to roast the pig," said Justice White.

In its decision, the Court reiterated its distinction between that which is merely indecent and protected by the First Amendment and that which is obscene and not so protected. But, said Justice White, "the case before us does not require us to decide what is obscene and what is indecent." Although the Court did not feel called on to distinguish between what was obscene and indecent, it would be a mistake to jump to the conclusion that the Court is opposed to any form of regulation. Instead it made clear that Congress could direct the Federal Communications Commission to regulate rather than ban indecent telephone messages so as to restrict access by minors. Inasmuch as Congress is in no better position to know where to draw the line between an obscenity that is not protected by the First Amendment and an indecency that is, there will be continued ambiguity and litigation in this area.

## Freedom of Expression in the Movies

Determining what is obscene is perhaps more difficult in plays and movies than in any other form of expression. As recently as 1969, one Southern city declared obscene a film about black and white children playing together and banned it. In the same year, the Chicago Police Board of Censorship held a Walt Disney movie obscene because it showed a buffalo giving birth.

The official censor in New York is the Board of Regents, which saw nothing wrong with the film *The Moon Is Blue,* in which the words "virginity" and "pregnancy" were used. However, to viewers from the United States Navy and the state of Maryland, the film was considered lewd and was banned. New York banned the film *Lady Chatterly's Lover,* only to have the decision overturned by the United States Supreme Court (*Kingsley International Pictures v. Regents,* 1957). That the movies were entitled to the protection of the First Amendment was, however, something not originally contemplated by Congress or the courts.

When the motion picture industry was in its infancy, the movies were considered merely another spectacle, like professional boxing or the circus. In *Mutual Film Corporation v. Industrial Commission of Ohio* (1915), the Court held that exhibiting motion pictures "is a business, pure and simple ... and is not to be regarded as part of the press or as organs of public opinion." As in the earliest days of the printing press, motion picture studios could be required to obtain a license; in the case of film, the First Amendment was deemed inapplicable.

What may have been true in 1915 was clearly absurd by the 1950s. Motion pictures such as *Ten Days That Shook the World*, *The Grapes of Wrath* and *All Quiet on the Western Front*, among many others, provided ample proof that the movies were doing more than entertaining. They were molding public opinion, contributing to the store of knowledge and disseminating ideas, some of which were provocative; they were becoming an art form. That the movies were entitled to First Amendment protection was a position taken by the Supreme Court in *Burstyn v. Wilson* in 1952.

This case involved a 40-minute Italian-language movie directed by Roberto Rossellini, entitled *The Miracle*, which the Catholic Church held was blasphemous. New York, where the film was shown, requires all commercially produced films to obtain a license, which they are granted if they are not obscene, immoral, crime-inciting or sacrilegious. After giving *The Miracle* a license, the Board of Regents reversed itself and revoked the license on the ground that the film cast doubt on the Biblical account of the conception of Jesus. In its decision, the Court reversed its 1915 position by declaring that films are to be protected by the First Amendment. While it did not rule out prior restraint altogether, this was to be the rare exception rather than the rule. In 1975, the Court ruled that the live musical *Hair* was entitled to the constitutional safeguards against prior restraint that are applicable to newspapers, books and movies. As a result of these and other decisions, prior restraint as a form of censoring plays and movies has become extremely rare. However, some local ordinances persist, and films that are believed to be obscene may still be challenged in court after they are shown.

Since 1980, movie houses specializing in pornographic films have been rapidly going out of business. However, with videocasettes readily available for sale or rent, pornography has moved into the home. In 1969, in the case of *Stanley v. Georgia*, the Supreme Court recognized that community standards of obscenity could not be applied to home entertainment. Justice Thurgood Marshall wrote, "If the First Amendment means anything, it means that a State has no business telling a man, sitting alone in his house, what books he may read or what films he may watch. Our whole constitutional heritage rebels at the thought of giving government the power to control men's minds."

Despite these safeguards, movies remain the most censored medium of expression in America because children make up so much of the audience for motion pictures and the Supreme Court has upheld regulations forbidding the sale of obscene material to children. In an attempt to regulate itself, the movie industry has adopted a system of self-censorship that evaluates films in terms of their suitability for children. The current classifications are as follows:

| | |
|---|---|
| G | General audiences, all ages admitted |
| PG | Parental Guidance suggested, all ages admitted |
| PG-13 | Parental Guidance strongly suggested, all ages admitted |
| R | Restricted, no one under the age of 18 admitted without an adult guardian |
| X | No person under 18 admitted |

In reaching these classifications, the industry evaluates not only the sexually explicit content of the film but also such factors as nudity, language and the level of gore, bloodshed and violence.

While the movie industry regulates what can or cannot be shown on the big screen, television, too, has a set of standards that must be met before material can be aired. In the next chapter, we'll learn how the First Amendment applies to the broadcast media.

# CHAPTER SIX

# Free Speech on the Air

When the First Amendment was written, the only forms of communication were what the human mouth could utter and what the human hand could write or put into print. How to apply the traditions of a free press to movies, radio, television, computers—in short, the entire range of telecommunications, all of which have become so prevalent and powerful—remains an unsettled question.

## The Tower of Babel

The First Amendment, which forbids Congress from abridging freedom of speech, explicitly states that Congress can make no law prohibiting freedom of the press. Had radio, telephone, television and film existed in the early days of the American republic, would the First Amendment then read, "Congress shall make no law abridging freedom of speech, press, radio, telephone, computers, FAX machines, television and film?" Would Thomas Jefferson become the champion of freedom of expression had he visualized the many forms of mass electronic communication by which men and women of our planet communicate with one another?

The Bible tells us that after the Flood the descendants of Noah tried to build a tower that would reach heaven, and God punished them for their presumption by confusing their languages. Because of their inability to communicate with one another, the Tower of Babel was never built. Today, not only do people speak in many tongues but there are many more ways of communicating than merely by word of mouth or print. Parallel confusion reigns in applying the values of the First Amendment to means of communication of which the Founding Fathers could not even dream.

In the Communication Act of 1934, Congress specifically included broadcasting as form of communication covered by the word *speech* as used in the First Amendment. Congress recognized, however, that communicating through the electronic media appeared to require special treatment, different from that accorded to the conventional press. At least so it seemed to those who drafted the legislation in the early days of radio. As a result, words broadcast through the electronic media are more strictly regulated than words in print. Compared with street-corner oratory or with magazines and newspapers, radio and television are far more limited in their freedom of expression. But is this fair? Need the words of the electronic media be more closely controlled than the spoken or written word? This chapter explores some of the dimensions of this complicated question.

## Licensed to Talk

The first broadcasting station, KDKA, operated by the Westinghouse Company, was opened in East Pittsburgh on November 2, 1920. It carried the first broadcast of national election returns when it reported the Harding-Cox victory.

Listening to radio—to music, to sermons and later to sportscasts—became a national obsession. In this way, a more sophisticated form of national communication rapidly grew.

In the early days of the American republic, a pamphlet, a handbill or a speech in a public square were all important ways by which people could be informed and public opinion could be influenced. Those with a little money and a lot of courage could, under these circumstances, express themselves as they wished. But radio was much more complex.

As discussed in Chapter One, for nearly 200 years after printing was first invented, the British government insisted that a license be obtained before one could open a shop to print newspapers, books, pamphlets, handbills and so on. The purpose of licensing was to ensure that what was printed did not question the authority of the monarch. However, because such licensing became widely recognized as a form of prior restraint and as such inconsistent with the growth of democracy, the practice of requiring licenses for printing was gradually abandoned. Today, no license to open a print shop or begin a newspaper or magazine is required. This is not so with radio or television.

Almost from its earliest days, licenses were required for the establishment of a radio station. Initially, the justification for requiring such a license was that the number of stations that could broadcast at one time was limited; licenses were required so that the stations would not interfere with each other's programs. While print and paper are essentially in unlimited supply, the airwaves were thought to be strictly limited. For that reason, even though speech was protected by the First Amendment, a radio station and later a television station had to have a license before it could allow anyone to speak on the air. In his last opinion as an Appeals Court judge before becoming Chief Justice, Warren Burger held that while "A newspaper can be operated at the whim or caprice of its owner, a broadcast station cannot." (*Office of Communications of the United Church of Christ v. FCC*, 1966.)

When the Federal Radio Commission was established in 1927, its purpose was to maintain control over all the channels and to grant short-term licenses to "worthy" applicants. But there was always a question of how to measure worthiness. Furthermore, radio stations and television channels must serve the public interest in order to have their licenses renewed periodically, but newspapers, magazine and other print media have no such obligations.

The licensing of radio and television was further justified by what was believed to be the greater impact of these media on listeners and viewers. There has been great concern that sexually explicit themes or excessive violence could scar the minds or warp the attitudes of children. Should such material be offered? It is a debate that rages on today.

Even though licensing implied prior restraint, a practice essentially discarded as applied to the print media, it remains an acceptable practice in the electronic media. When the Federal Communications Commission was established in 1934 to regulate radio, telephone and eventually television, the practice of requiring a license in order to broadcast was continued. However, the FCC was explicitly prohibited from censoring what was aired—the only exceptions being that which was obscene, indecent or profane.

Although the FCC is forbidden to censor, there is little question that there are far more restrictions for radio and television than there are for newspapers and magazines. Radio stations and television channels must meet certain standards before their licenses can be renewed. They must, for example, provide a reasonable amount of time to inform the public on controversial issues. They must also see to it that many shades of view on these controversial issues are presented.

In the case of *Red Lion Broadcasting Company v. FCC* (1969), the United States Supreme Court held that broadcasters "act as proxies for an entire community." It was in this case that the "fairness doctrine" joined its close cousin, the "equal time doctrine," as guidelines for radio and television broadcasters. According to the first, radio and television had to be "fair" to all or to at least a reasonable number of points of view. According to the second, radio and television had to make available equal time to viable candidates for public office. In the electronic media, licensing, fairness and equal time have become controversial to the extent that these principles clash with freedom of expression on the one hand and with emerging technology on the other. These issues have been called into question with increasing vigor.

## To License or Not to License?

In order to broadcast, radio and television stations must obtain a license from the Federal Communications Commission. If the stations have complied with FCC regulations, the licenses are renewed every three years. Because the FCC can revoke a license, to the radio and television industry the FCC is "big brother," constantly looking over their shoulder and monitoring their performance. While the FCC is clearly and explicitly prohibited from censoring what the radio and television stations choose to air, the very idea that a license can be revoked has a chilling effect on what the stations choose to do or refrain from doing.

As a realistic matter, however, keeping a license is not difficult. What a station has to do is to present a rough idea of what it intends to broadcast—how much will be entertainment, how much news, how much public service and how much talk. Stations are expected to perform in accordance with the plans they submit, but there is a good deal of flexibility in them. The

FCC does not control the quality of what is put on the air. It makes no judgment; the talk shows may be repetitive, the entertainment dull, the news superficial. Nor does the FCC insist that what the television or radio stations air be accurate or even truthful except in rare occasions where the news is excessively slanted or even staged. The FCC will insist, however, that on controversial issues radio and television be fair to conflicting sides. Even here, the FCC takes a rather detached attitude and does not enforce fairness rigidly. But the "fairness doctrine" by itself is a controversial question.

While losing a license is rare, the need to apply for renewal every three years remains a threat that modifies the selection and content of the programs radio and television broadcast. It gives government officials at all levels clout over what radio and television do, clout that they do not have over unlicensed newspapers or magazines. The major television stations are particularly sensitive to the complaints of Congress and the executive branch of government. When a television station, for example, airs a program critical of a branch of government, those who feel offended can harass the networks or their affiliated stations by asking for supporting data and requesting that the networks explain how they reached their conclusions. This requires the services of a large full-time staff whose only function is to respond to even the most trivial question those in authority ask.

From the point of view of the news departments, even the hypothetical power to renew or revoke licenses means that time-consuming and expensive procedures must be in place to defend their programs. Sometimes, using the licensing club, a "war of nerves" can be created between the networks and their affiliates. Because of the potential burden of answering a host of questions, some radio and television stations may choose to avoid airing controversial issues altogether. In part, it is because of the burden of justifying what they air in ways that no newspaper would dream of doing that television has rarely become the medium through which major domestic and international questions are probed in depth. It is, however, the major news source for the majority of Americans.

Richard Salant, then president of CBS news, declared in a *New York Times* article on May 6, 1971, that because of licensing "... Government intervention and coercion can take a multitude of sinister forms other than naked censorship." These comments were made during Richard Nixon's term as president, when the relations between the administration and the media were particularly hostile; nevertheless, licensing does seem to offer the potential for indirect censorship of radio and television news and commentary.

Licensing in America was based on the assumption that the electronic media were not entitled to the full range of First Amendment protection available to newspapers and magazines. Technological developments, however, are blurring the distinction between print and the electronic media. If information is made available on a computer screen or FAX machine and if print material is transmitted via television, do all the privileges of the First Amendment apply, or only some of them? Because electronic and print media are drawing closer together, how should the First Amendment be applied?

In general, three responses have been made to this question, but no consensus has been reached on any of them.

One view insists that we have the best of both worlds by having a totally free press and a quasi-free electronic media. In this duality, one can check and balance the other while the citizen has access to both media, albeit in different ways. The print media are essentially unrestrained and can take sharp and pointed positions on controversial issues. The press need not be fair nor print all sides of a question if it chooses not to do so. The electronic media need to be more cautious so that all sides of an issue are fairly treated. According to this view, such a requirement ensures that the public has access to views that may not find their way into print. While government regulation in the form of licensing does inhibit freedom of expression, the unrestrained and unregulated press provides sharp competition and encourages electronic broadcasters to be bold.

Another view holds that as print and broadcast journalism become indistinguishable from one another, the former should be licensed as is the latter. Those holding this position insist that the concept that the press provides a "free market" for the expression of opinion is largely a romantic myth. If it was ever true that those with even a modest print shop could start a newspaper, it is no longer the case.

Instead, a great deal of capital is needed to launch a newspaper or magazine. Therefore, while frequencies may be limited for radio and TV broadcasting, so access to newspapers is likewise limited. Evidence for this may be seen in the smaller number of newspapers available in almost every city in the country. In 1987, there were but 1,645 newspapers in the United States. Whereas many communities once were served by both morning and evening newspapers, today more and more cities have just a single morning edition.

In view of the relatively limited number of newspapers, should they not also be required to be "fair" and to provide space for views contrary to those of the newspaper's ownership? And if in order to achieve this goal newspapers need to be licensed so as to monitor their compliance, would not the model of the broadcast media be appropriate?

A third position insists that neither the electronic nor the print media should be licensed. Those holding this view insist that the initial reason for licensing radio and television, namely, the limited availability of frequencies, is rapidly disappearing. The development of cable television and, on the horizon, interactive television (in which the audience can respond to queries or even participate by asking questions) makes the original reason for requiring licensing largely outmoded.

Because there are more television stations in the United States than there are newspapers, television should be free from some of the onerous inhibitions imposed upon it. Because there are many television options available and many more growing, television too should be able to take sides and develop strong editorial positions. Those who disagree with one station's opinions can view one of literally hundreds of other channels. Owning a television station of one's own may not be realistic, but it is not realistic today to think in terms of owning a newspaper of one's own either.

This view has deep historic roots. That is, each time a new medium of communication was made available, the extension of democracy was encouraged. When the papyrus of ancient Egypt replaced writing in stone, the public could be more widely informed. When paper replaced papyrus, as it did in medieval Europe, a further extension of information was made possible. Today, more people are informed through broadcast journalism than through any other means.

The development of the electronic media opens up the United States and indeed the world to rapid and instant communication, making our society a "global village" in which international and local news and gossip may come just as readily from Picadilly Circus in London, from the Place de la Concorde in Paris, from the Kremlin in Moscow or from Tiananmen Square in Beijing as from Times Square in New York. Over the next decade, the demands for more democracy and greater freedom of expression and the imperatives of emerging technology will encourage the abandonment of licensing of the electronic media and the extension to radio and television journalism the full privileges of the First Amendment now accorded newspapers and magazines.

## Walking the Tightrope: The Fairness Doctrine

Suppose the sole newspaper of a community chose to print only antiabortion arguments. What remedy would the pro-choice advocates have? The answer is none at all. If, however, a television station presented the antiabortion position for five minutes, it would have an obligation to present the pro-choice position for a similar amount of time. The newspaper can take the position it does because it enjoys the full protection of the First Amendment and so is free of government regulation. The television station must take the position it does because it is required to do so by FCC regulation. As a result, the broadcast media walk a tightrope upon which they balance First Amendment values of freedom of speech with government regulations that insist that presentations be fair.

The "fairness doctrine" was formally adopted by the Federal Communications Commission in 1949. It was endorsed 10 years later by Congress in an amendment to the Communications Act. Under the doctrine radio and television stations were obligated, in order to get and keep their licenses, to broadcast in the public interest. That interest required fairness (1) by devoting a reasonable amount of time to controversial issues facing the general public and (2) by allowing contrasting opinions to be aired. By itself, the statement does not appear to be unreasonable. However, its application generates a great deal of controversy and uncertainty among the public and the broadcasters and is troublesome to scholars of the First Amendment.

It was not until 1967, however, in *Red Lion Broadcasting Co., Inc., v. FCC,* that the Supreme Court clearly endorsed the fairness doctrine for the electronic media. On the afternoon of November 25, 1964, Reverend Billy James Hargis was on radio station WGCB-AM/FM of Red Lion, Pennsylvania, when he lashed out against Fred J. Cook, an investigative reporter who had taken critical aim at Richard Nixon, Barry Goldwater, J. Edgar Hoover and the religious right. In an article in the magazine *The Nation*, Cook had classified Hargis as a bigot. Hargis, on the radio, shot back by calling Cook "a professional mudslinger." The Hargis attack lasted two minutes and cost $7.50 in air time. Using the fairness doctrine as a wedge, Mr. Cook demanded an opportunity to reply to the Hargis charge.

FCC rules required that the time be made available without charge if the speaker could not find a sponsor or otherwise pay for the time. Fred Cook called upon the FCC to enforce its own rules and require WGCB to make free time available to him. The 83-year-old owner of Red Lion refused to comply and took his case to the court of appeals in Washington, D.C. That court upheld the FCC rules on the fairness doctrine. Thus encouraged, the FCC elaborated on its rules by more precisely stating the obligations of broadcasters when personal attacks have been made.

Other broadcasters took up the issue by attacking the fairness doctrine, especially the new and more complicated rules the FCC imposed. The Radio-Television News Directors Association, later joined by NBC and CBS, took the case to the Seventh Circuit Court of Appeals in Chicago. Here the broadcasters won in a unanimous decision. The court of appeals held that the right of reply to personal attack collided "... with free-speech and free-press guarantees contained in the First Amendment." The *News Directors* case and the *Red Lion* case were consolidated and were heard by the United States Supreme Court, which in 1967 ruled in favor of the FCC by upholding both the "personal attack" rule and the fairness doctrine. Cook was offered 15 free minutes by Red Lion Broadcasting, but he declined, claiming that after the long period of time that had elapsed the issues about which they were debating had become irrelevant.

In its decision, the Supreme Court held: "Congress ... forbids FCC interference with the right of free speech by means of radio communication [but] it is the right of viewers and listeners, not the right of the broadcaster which is paramount." In effect, the listeners' and viewers' right to be informed, to know, was more important than the broadcasters' right to choose what to broadcast. The collective good of society was placed ahead of the freedom-of-speech rights of the broadcasters.

A startlingly different interpretation is placed on the First Amendment as it applies to print. In *Miami Herald Publishing Co. v. Tornillo* (1974), the Court held: "The choice of material to go into a newspaper ... [the] treatment of public issues and public officials—whether fair or unfair—constitute the exercise of editorial control and judgment. It has yet to be demonstrated how governmental regulation of this crucial process can be exercised consistent with First Amendment guarantees of a free press. ..."

In the case of electronic media, the value of government regulation to encourage the rights of viewers and listeners to know, to be informed, was preferred to the absolute application of the First Amendment. In the case of the print media, the First Amendment value of a free press was accorded priority over the public's right to know.

Twenty years after *Red Lion*, while the full applicability of the First Amendment has yet to be applied to radio and television, the fairness doctrine was abandoned by the FCC. Because of new technology, the public could be informed by the mere existence of many more television channels, and the fairness doctrine seemed to be no longer in the public interest. The FCC recognized that the requirement of fair presentation of controversial issues might even inhibit broadcasters, who had become reluctant to present issues of public controversy lest they get bogged down in litigation alleging that some facet of the issue had been ignored or given short shrift. The FCC now saw in the fairness doctrine a chilling effect on the rights of broadcast journalists.

## Equal Time

The equal time doctrine is a close cousin of the fairness doctrine. Fairness concerns itself with controversial issues and the content of news and public affairs programs; equal time concerns itself with how to apportion broadcast time among candidates for public office. The equal time rule is more precise in that it requires broadcasters to give equal treatment to candidates for public office who must be sold or given equal opportunity to promote their candidacy on the air. Moreover, it is not enough for broadcasters to make equal time available to official candidates; they must also give the candidates equal access to the prime time slots. Fees charged candidates must be the same as those charged other advertisers and, as with other advertisers, candidates are entitled to quantity discounts.

Controversy sometimes arises when a candidate is featured in a newscast, news interview or on-the-spot coverage or in a documentary. In such cases, is the candidate's opponent then entitled to the equal opportunity to air his or her rebuttal? A documentary about a candidate usually requires a radio or television station to give equal time to opposing candidates. However, in the case of a news documentary in which the candidate's appearance is incidental to the subject being covered, equal time does not apply.

The Nixon-Kennedy debates of 1960 were made possible when Congress temporarily suspended the equal time provision (Section 325 of the Communications Act). Suspension was necessary because a strict interpretation of the equal time provision would have meant that every minor self-proclaimed candidate for the presidency would likewise have to be given the chance to debate.

While it cannot be said that the press is free and the broadcast media unfree, nevertheless the latter work under limitations that are no longer applicable to the former. Perhaps what is still needed is a case that would do for the electronic media what the Zenger case did for print. In the Zenger case, truth was accepted as a defense against seditious libel and the development of an uninhibited press was encouraged. But as we've seen in this book, the values of unconstrained speech and press may clash with the values of those who wish to be protected from personal slurs, the obscene, the sexually explicit and the pornographic. In such a confrontation, where should the line be drawn?

CHAPTER SEVEN

# Demonstrating for Change

Have you ever written to your teacher or principal to ask for better food in the lunchroom? If so, you are exercising your right to "petition for redress of grievances" as guaranteed in the First Amendment. By signing a letter or other communication in which you and many others collectively ask for an improvement in the way garbage is collected in your neighborhood or the way the police protect a park, you are likewise taking advantage of your constitutional right to petition. Anyone in government, high or low, may be so petitioned, from the president of the United States to a member of the Cabinet, the Senate or House of Representatives or your state and local officials.

If you receive no response to your petition, if you're dissatisfied with that response or if there is no improvement in the matter about which you complain, you are free to join with others to determine what further steps you may wish to take. This "right of the people peaceably to assemble" is likewise guaranteed by the First Amendment. The right to assemble peaceably and to petition government is as fundamental to a democracy as freedom of speech and the press.

## "I Am the Law"

At one time, merely communicating with a ruler for any purpose whatsoever was regarded as an affront at best and subversive at worst. When the citizens of Massachusetts in 1767 and 1768 petitioned King George III in protest against the taxes on tea, they were severely rebuked by the king and by Parliament for having the presumption to address the monarch. Their act was regarded as treasonous, and those who had lent their names to the petition were in peril. In 1774, when the members of the First Continental Congress enumerated their grievances, they asserted that their rights as English people had been violated when the Crown refused to hear their petition.

In the United States, the right to petition, assemble and associate has had to be defended anew many times. Between 1840 and 1845, the House of Representatives refused to accept antislavery petitions. During the depression of 1893–1894, J. S. Coxey led his "army" of unemployed to Washington, D.C., to petition for a program that would put the jobless to work. The demonstrators were arrested for trespassing on the grass of the Capitol. In 1932, a "Bonus Army" of soldiers also marched on Washington, D.C., demanding immediate payment of the bonus they believed due them as means of relieving their plight during the depression. They were forcibly expelled from their camps by federal tanks and troops under the leadership of General Douglas MacArthur.

In times of stress—when the nation was founded, when slavery was a burning issue in American life, during severe economic downturns—the right to assemble peaceably is under pressure. Whenever emotional men and women on opposing sides of important issues confront each other, violence may ensue. The First Amendment explicitly limits the right to assemble only to those who are peaceable and lawful, but how may communities ensure that this will in fact be the case?

Before he was elevated to the United States Supreme Court, Oliver Wendell Holmes rendered an opinion for the Supreme Judicial Court of Massachusetts in which he said that a municipality can regulate its streets and parks the way a person can regulate his or her home. That is, just as an individual may invite some people into the home and not others, so a community may allow some people to meet and not allow others to do so. This decision was upheld in 1897 by the United States Supreme Court. While frequently challenged, it was not overturned until the Supreme Court ruled in case of *Hague v. Committee for Industrial Organization* in 1939.

The 1930s were years of stress. During the nation's most severe depression, American workers sought to organize themselves into labor unions in order to fight more effectively for higher wages, shorter hours and safer working conditions. In order to gain the strength to be able to bargain collectively with their employers, they needed to hold outdoor rallies and meetings in public places to arouse the enthusiasm of workers and urge them to form labor unions.

Many local communities denied permission for these meetings, especially in the highly industrialized states. In New Jersey, for example, ordinances against outdoor meetings for some groups were enforced with a heavy hand by Mayor Frank Hague of Jersey City, who imperiously boasted, "I am the law."

He meant that no group could meet in "his" city unless it had a permit obtained three days in advance from his director of public safety. That official could deny such a permit if there was some chance that "a riot, disturbance, or disorderly assemblage" might result from those who were opposed to the meeting. If a group of workers sought to meet in a Jersey City park, for instance, and the businesspeople in the local Chamber of Commerce threatened violence, the permit could be denied and the workers could not meet.

While these regulations had their heaviest impact against workers, others too were prevented from assembling. The editor of the *Catholic Worker*, W. M. Callahan, who sought to hold a meeting to explain papal encyclicals, was denied permission. United States Senator William Borah could not hold a meeting, nor could the Socialist leader Norman Thomas. In nearby Paterson, New Jersey, Roger Baldwin, the head of the American Civil Liberties Union, was promptly arrested when he endeavored to read from the Declaration of Independence in a public square.

### *Hague v. Committee for Industrial Organization* (1939)

When the Committee for Industrial Organization (CIO) sought to hold a meeting in Jersey City, permission was denied because there was fear that the opposition of a number of organizations, including the Chamber of Commerce, two veterans' groups and the Ladies of the Grand Army of the Republic, might lead to riots. When the CIO took its case through the courts, there was evidence that Mayor Hague had encouraged at least some of the protests. This led the federal circuit court to remark, "Reversing the usual procedure, Mayor Hague troubled the waters in order to fish in them." The Supreme Court finally declared the Jersey City ordinances void. Mayor Hague and his city administration acquiesced, and meetings in public places were held unhindered.

Because meetings must still be peaceably held for lawful purposes, governments may still impose rules and regulations on how the community's streets and parks may be used. The Jersey City ordinances were objectionable because they were arbitrary and could be applied to any meeting for which there was likely to be opposition. In practical terms, it is hard to find a meeting to which there would be no objection from any group. But in order to ensure peaceable assembly, orderly parades and nonviolent rallies, a city may regulate outdoor meetings so as to make sure that such events minimize disruption in the daily life of the community. Parades and demonstrations may be confined to certain areas in order to minimize interference with traffic or with the recreational needs of nonparticipating citizens. These regulations must be reasonable: fair to all who wish to assemble lawfully and peaceably. Because public meetings contribute to a democratic society, such proper regulations should have the effect of making outdoor facilities available without discrimination to all groups who may want to use them.

## The Right of Assembly

In the 1939 case of *Hague v. CIO*, a Bill of Rights Committee of the American Bar Association was formed to intervene in the case as a friend of the court. In its brief, the committee produced a lengthy explanation of the importance of freedom of assembly. The committee drew on *DeJonge v. Oregon* (1937), in which the Supreme Court recognized the intimate relationship between the right to assemble and petition and the rights of freedom of speech and the press.

DeJonge had been convicted by the state of Oregon and sentenced to jail for seven years for speaking at a rally of the Communist Party. The Court held that DeJonge's imprisonment was unconstitutional and that the constitutional rights of free speech, press and assembly are indispensable if government is to be responsive to the people's will.

The Bill of Rights Committee, in considering the New Jersey cases, confined its comments mainly to the outdoor meetings that had been the target of the Jersey City ordinances. Such meetings, the committee asserted, are a traditional part of American life. Today, despite advanced technology, a great many meetings involving discussion of political, social and economic questions still take place outdoors.

The outdoors offers free space, convenient locations and opportunities for face-to-face confrontation. The informality of the outdoor meeting lends itself effectively to questions and answers, and is in many ways the most democratic form of expression.

"The right of assembly lies at the foundation of our system of government," the members of the Bill of Rights Committee insisted. It is through public assembly that men and women can be informed and the uncoerced consent of the governed achieved. But do local municipalities "own" the streets and parks as a person "owns" a house? Although the Supreme Court had decided that such was the case, the Bill of Rights Committee believed the Court, in this instance, to be in error. The committee argued that while people own houses for their own use, streets and parks are for public use. It is the responsibility of a municipality to make them available to the people; the city can regulate but it cannot discriminate.

But what of the requirement that assembly be peaceable? While it is understood that meetings must not lead to riot or violence, it is often impossible to judge the outcome of a meeting in advance. To do so is to impose prior restraint, which is against the law in matters of freedom of speech and the press as well as freedom of assembly. A meeting must not be forbidden or broken up unless a real disturbance of the peace arises, for to do so would be to suppress every form of public discussion. Instead, communities must make appropriate police protection available without discrimination to those who wish to meet. And, quoting Justice Louis Brandeis from an earlier decision, "Those who won our independence by revolution were not cowards. ... They did not exalt order at the cost of liberty."

The intervention by the Committee for the Bill of Rights helped overturn the procedures Jersey City imposed on open-air assemblies. The decision altered the way cities managed their parks and streets and by so doing made them more widely available for public demonstrations and for the sharing of ideas and the forming of opinion.

## "I Have a Dream"

The Constitution of the United States says nothing about the right of men and women to form permanent associations with one another in order to pursue a common purpose. But inasmuch as the right of association is nothing more than the right to assemble on a long-term and organized basis, association is likewise protected. When the National Association of Colored People (NAACP) refused the state of Alabama's demand to turn over its membership list, the Supreme Court ruled that the NAACP need not do so. In its decision, *NAACP v. Alabama* (1958), Justice Harlan wrote, "It is beyond debate that freedom to engage in association for the advancement of beliefs and ideas is an inseparable part of liberty ... ."

Groups that organize themselves to pursue common interests are called lobbies. They consist of men and women outside of government who try to influence Congress to vote for legislation they believe will help them. The term *lobby* comes from the fact that much of the negotiation and "arm twisting" of the legislators is done in the corridors or lobbies of Congress. There are thousands of lobbies for all kinds of special-interest purposes. Some oppose abortion, some support it, others favor gun control, some do not. Industry, labor, agriculture all have offices in Washington, D.C., where they work on behalf of the interests of those who support them. Their right to do so is protected by the right to peaceably assemble and petition government.

It was under the protection of the First Amendment that the March on Washington took place on August 28, 1963. More than 200,000 people heard Reverend Martin Luther King Jr. deliver a moving address in which he said, "I have a dream that one day the nation will rise up and live out the true meaning of its creed ... all men are created equal." A year later, President Lyndon Johnson signed the Civil Rights Act of 1964 and later the Voting Rights Act of 1965. These measures have reshaped American politics in countless ways, especially in our nation's long struggle for civil rights

### "My Feet Were Tired"

On December 1, 1955, Rosa Parks left the Montgomery, Alabama, department store in which she worked as a seamstress and took her regular bus home. It would be a bus ride that would mark a detour in history.

Rosa Parks, a well-known and respected member of the black community of Montgomery and a secretary of the local chapter of the NAACP, boarded the bus and took her seat in the first row of the section reserved for blacks. However, as the bus filled up, the driver stopped the vehicle and, exercising the authority granted him by the local segregation laws of the city, ordered the four blacks in the first rowof the black section to give up their seats for whites.

Even though they would have to stand, three of the blacks complied, as was expected of them. But Rosa Parks's feet were tired, and she refused to budge. She denied the bus driver's demand that she give up her seat in a voice that could barely be heard above the purring motor of the bus. But she remained adamant in her refusal to move, and she was arrested and imprisoned. By doing so, she launched a movement that rocked the world.

For the new minister at the Dexter Avenue Baptist Church, the year-long boycott of the Montgomery buses that followed began his career as a nonviolent crusader for an end to racism in the United States. In his initial speech on the subject, the Reverend Martin Luther King Jr. told his assembled audience, "There comes a time when people get tired of being trampled over by the iron feet of oppression. ... We are here because we are tired now. ... The only weapon we have in our hands this evening is the weapon of protest. If we were incarcerated behind the iron curtains of a communistic nation—we couldn't do this. If we were trapped in the dungeon of a totalitarian regime—we couldn't do this. But the great glory of American democracy is the right to protest for right ... ."

"The right to protest for right" is deeply rooted. The Reverend William Sloane Coffin reminds us that "Moses was a wanted man, and David an outlaw" and that Jesus and his disciples transgressed both civil and religious law. Socrates, Thoreau, Gandhi and King all defied the law when the law conflicted with their consciences. Those who settled in the New World were religious dissenters; people like Anne Hutchinson and William Rogers broke the religious laws of their communities and were banished for their efforts.

The Founding Fathers of the nation defied the British Stamp Tax, dumped tea in Boston harbor and proclaimed their independence from England. Many Americans defied the Fugitive Slave Laws, which required that runaway slaves be returned to their masters. Some formed "underground railways" in order to establish escape routes from the South to safe haven in the North or in Canada. Labor leaders often disobeyed laws in order to secure the right to bargain collectively with corporate management. There are many more examples of heroism on the part of men and women who defied the law when the law clashed with conscience.

The 1960s was a decade of a great deal of dissent and protest in America. In protesting for what they believed was right, many dissidents defied local or national laws in order to obtain what they perceived to be a more just or humane society. Some of the more significant protests of the 1960s were the following:

In 1960, four black students at North Carolina A and T College held a sit-in at a lunch counter and began a campaign to end segregation in eating places.

In 1961, "Freedom Rides" began to test segregated interstate transportation facilities, including waiting rooms and rest rooms.

In 1962, a peace march of students was held in Washington, D.C. James Meredith tried to integrate the University of Mississippi.

In 1963, Dr. Martin Luther King Jr. led 200,000 demonstrators in a march on Washington, D.C.

In 1964, civil-rights workers James Chaney, Andrew Goodman and Michael Schwerner were beaten and shot to death in Mississippi. The "free speech movement" turned the Berkeley campus of the University of California into turmoil.

In 1966, James Meredith was killed in ambush while urging blacks to register and vote.

In 1967, Martin Luther King Jr. called on men and women "of conscience" to boycott the Vietnam War.

In 1968, Martin Luther King Jr. was assassinated in Memphis, Tennessee, where he had gone to help sanitation workers in their strike. Students seized a number of buildings at Columbia University in New York. In Catonsville, Maryland, the Reverends Philip and Daniel Berrigan were arrested for burning draft records and Dr. Benjamin Spock and the Reverend William Sloane Coffin were indicted for conspiracy to encourage draft evasion. Robert Kennedy, a candidate for President of the United States, was also assassinated.

In 1970, National Guardsmen shot and killed four students on the campus of Kent State University.

## Civil Disobedience

In his stirring speech launching the Montgomery, Alabama, bus boycott, King declared, "There will be nobody among us who will stand up and defy the Constitution of this nation." In view of this pledge, was it right for Rosa Parks to defy a lawful city ordinance and refuse to move to the back of the bus? In a government based on the consent of the governed, if the people, through their democratically chosen representatives, agree on a law, does anyone have a right to disobey it? Does each individual have the right to determine which laws are just and which are not, which laws he or she will obey and which not?

The right to assemble peaceably implies the right of men and women to gather together to protest unjust laws. In such protests the assemblage often defies laws the community has democratically adopted. Nonviolent civil disobedience against unjust laws was used by Mahatma Gandhi to secure independence for India. It was a philosophy later used by Reverend Martin Luther King Jr. to dismantle segregation in the United States and to secure voting rights for blacks. During the war in Vietnam, it was used by opponents of that war to defy the draft and to attempt to shorten the war by protesting American involvement. Students resorted to nonviolence not only to protest the Vietnam War but also to secure rights for blacks and other minorities, including women and homosexuals.

Nonviolent civil disobedience implies that at times a higher morality justifies defying rather than obeying unjust or inhuman laws. Each generation has had to wrestle with the moral dilemma of civil disobedience. Let us see some of the arguments on either side of the issue.

**Civil Disobedience Is Wrong**

In ancient Athens, Socrates wrestled with the question of whether or not to try to escape the death sentence imposed upon him. He resisted the blandishments of friends who urged him to escape by saying that men and women have an obligation to the state. "... the state ... has nurtured and educated us, ... has provided the amenities of life for you and me and for every other citizen. By remaining here and taking advantage of these opportunities haven't we entered into at least an implied contract to obey the laws of the state? Aren't we obligated to obey its laws?"

Those who oppose civil disobedience insist that in a democratic nation disobeying even bad laws is wrong. Instead, men and women should work through the processes made available through a democracy to change laws that are unjust, inequitable or immoral. In some societies, as in Nazi Germany, where no opportunity existed to change bad laws, disobedience to the state was the moral thing to do. But in the United States, where there are many opportunities to change the law, civil disobedience is never justified.

Since there is no check or test to determine whether or not they are right, do those who believe a law is immoral establish themselves as the sole judge of what is moral and what is not? If bad laws seem to limit the amount of housing or food available to the poor, does that justify blocking traffic, trespassing in a public place, harassing the police or disobeying other laws or ordinances that are, in themselves, far removed from the questions of housing or hunger?

There are some who insist that civil disobedience is appropriate if those who break the law are willing to take the consequences. That is, blocking traffic in order to demonstrate for a good cause may be unlawful, yet those truly committed to the techniques of nonviolent civil disobedience must not resist arrest and must be willing to go to jail instead. However, if one sets off the fire alarm, is it satisfactory atonement if one is prepared to go to jail for having done so? Lawlessness cannot be condoned simply because the lawbreaker is prepared to pay the penalty.

Civil disobedience thwarts the will of the majority, and to that extent it is elitist and undemocratic. Those who choose to disobey a law are always a few who try to prevail against the many. Moreover, if the best of people—those with a sincere commitment to a worthy cause—sanction civil disobedience for themselves, can they then deny it to the "worst" of people, say to members of the Ku Klux Klan? "To be revolutionary in a society like ours," wrote distinguished law professor Alexander M. Bickel, "is to be totalitarian, or not to know what one is doing."[1]

## Civil Disobedience Is Right

Those who hold the view that civil disobedience is right believe that, even in a government based on the consent of the governed, unjust laws are often passed. History is full of examples of instances in which the majority have acted unjustly. The existence of slavery for more than 200 years is a significant example of such majority-supported injustice in the United States. However, proponents of civil disobedience insist that even in a democracy only civil disobedience can bring about changes when other avenues have failed to do so. Civil disobedience superbly serves the needs of the minority, who have no other means of being heard. By definition, the majority sit athwart the very processes that have been constitutionally established to make change possible.

The Reverend William Sloane Coffin insists that while the law is worthy of respect, it is not deserving of unreasoning obedience. There is, in his view, a higher social goal than merely law and order, and the oppressed have a moral right to challenge oppressive laws. Moreover, they have an obligation to do so.

In our Constitution, there is no automatic procedure by which a law of Congress is reviewed for its constitutionality. For a judgment to be made about the constitutionality of a law, that law must be challenged in the courts, and in order to precipitate such a lawful challenge the law must first be disobeyed. This is primarily the view of Martin Luther King Jr., who challenged discriminatory, segregationist and racist legislation by violating the law (for example, by refusing to sit in the back of the bus). In such challenges, King often prevailed. Had he not challenged an unjust, discriminatory law in this way, it may have taken longer for the law to be declared unconstitutional.

Civil disobedience becomes more difficult when a law is clearly constitutional but is regarded as inhumane. Military conscription laws are good examples, especially when they are imposed during an unpopular war, such as the Vietnam War. Protesting these laws is where controversy over civil disobedience becomes most sharp. Often, in the process of disobeying a draft law, for instance, draft cards may be burned, offices may be entered, files may be destroyed. Those who support civil disobedience under these conditions insist that it is proper to violate a lesser law in order to achieve the abandonment of an unjust or inhumane one.

While civil disobedience should be peaceful and a last resort, it is often the only tool the weak have against the strong. It is the only way in which the conscience of the nation can be pricked so as to prevent lapses into stagnation and decay. There is a grave danger that the passionate intensity of zealots on some issues may outweigh rationality, pragmatism and compromise. Nevertheless, nonviolent civil disobedience may be thought of as an affirmative response to Cain's sullen outcry to God, "Am I my brother's keeper?"

CHAPTER EIGHT

# The Future of Free Speech

The First Amendment is a living document that needs constant nurturing to flourish. Each succeeding generation of Americans must take its turn at caring for freedom of speech, challenging laws that diminish it and fighting for the right to hear and to speak the truth. In the end, as Judge Learned Hand wrote in the early 1900s, liberty rests not in laws, but in the hearts and minds of people.

For young Americans, the fight for freedom of expression is often a difficult one. As the three cases discussed below show, many students take responsibility for the life of the First Amendment very seriously—sometimes at a very young age.

## *Tinker v. Des Moines Independent School District* (1969)

In December 1965, Mary Beth Tinker, a 13-year-old junior high school student in Des Moines, Iowa, wore a two-inch black armband to school to protest the Vietnam War. She was joined in this form of protest by her 16-year-old friend Christopher Eckhardt and the next day by her 15-year-old brother, John.

The protest, which was to last from December 16, 1965, to January 1, 1966, had the approval of Mary Beth's parents, who wore similar armbands to their jobs in a further expression of opposition to the war in Vietnam. But the wearing of armbands was viewed with alarm by the principal of the school and by other principals as well. They believed that wearing such armbands would encourage disruption of the orderly school day.

When the students were ordered to remove their armbands, they refused to do so. As a result, they were suspended and they did not return to school until January 1, when the demonstration was to end officially. The principals hoped that they had seen the end of the incident, but they were mistaken. The three students brought suit in federal court, claiming that their First Amendment rights had been violated.

The students lost in the federal district court but won on appeal to the United States Supreme Court in a vote of 7 to 2. A key portion of the *Tinker* decision held that public schools "may not be enclaves of totalitarianism." Young men and women do not lose their fundamental rights simply because they are students. Under our Constitution, they are entitled to express their views freely. Justice Abe Fortas, speaking for a majority of the Court, wrote, "It can hardly be argued that either students or teachers shed their constitutional rights to freedom of speech or expression at the schoolhouse gate."

The *Tinker* case paved the way for greater freedom of expression in our schools, but no decision of the Supreme Court can ensure that the guarantees of the First Amendment will not again be eroded in other schools, under other circumstances and other conditions. For those guarantees to remain meaningful for ourselves and our descendants, we need to know what they are, their extent and their limits.

## *Bethel School District No. 403 v. Fraser* (1986)

Matthew Fraser was an honor student at Bethel High School in the state of Washington. He was an especially fine public speaker and debater and had won a number of awards for speaking effectiveness. In April, 1983, Mr. Fraser delivered a one-minute nominating speech for a friend who was a candidate for the position of vice-president of the student body. One portion of the speech follows: "I know a man who is firm—he's firm in his pants, he's firm in his shirt, his character is firm—but most of all his belief, in you, the students of Bethel, is firm. Jeff Kuhlman is a man who takes his point and pounds on it. If necessary, he'll take an issue and nail it to the wall."[1]

Because the speech contained puns and double entendres, Mr. Fraser was suspended from school and his name removed from the list of students who were being considered as speakers at the Bethel High School commencement. School authorities insisted that Fraser had violated an important rule of the high school, which read: "Conduct which materially and substantially interferes with the educational process is prohibited, including the use of obscene, profane language or gestures."

Fraser served but two days of his suspension; after intervention by the United States district court in Washington, high school authorities were forced to allow Matthew to deliver the commencement address. The school administration appealed the ruling to the United States Court of Appeals, Ninth Circuit, which also decided for Fraser.

The school district appealed to the United States Supreme Court, which in July 1986 reversed the judgment of the lower courts. Chief Justice Warren Burger wrote the opinion for the majority. The Supreme Court held that schools were instruments of the state and "... may determine that the essential lessons of civil, mature conduct cannot be conveyed in a school that tolerates lewd, indecent, or offensive speech and conduct such as that indulged in by this confused boy. The pervasive sexual innuendo in Fraser's speech was plainly offensive to both teachers and students—indeed, to any mature person."

Justice Burger, in speaking for the Court, differentiated between the *Tinker* case, which seemed to expand the meaning of freedom of speech, and *Fraser*, which seemed to limit it. In *Tinker*, the First Amendment was involved because a political point of view was expressed. In *Fraser*, there was no such issue and so the First Amendment was not applicable. Moreover, according to the majority of the Supreme Court, the First Amendment in no way limits school officials from regulating vulgar speech. While the ruling in this case was not unanimous, as Justices Marshall and Stevens dissented, Justice Burger, in continuing to speak for the majority of the Court, held that "the process of educating our youth for citizenship in public schools is not confined to books, the curriculum and the civics class; school must teach by example the shared values of a civilized social order."

But in the *Fraser* case, what did the Supreme Court teach? Did it teach that the Constitution doesn't really mean what it says when Amendment One declares, "Congress shall make no law ... abridging freedom of speech ...?" Did the decision puncture young people's idealistic understanding of the meaning of democracy? Was the Court's decision in this case a reasonable limitation on freedom of expression? Are there such "reasonable" limitations?

## *Hazelwood School District v. Kuhlmeier* (1988)

"The educator's understandable ... mandate to inculcate moral and political values is not a general warrant to act as 'thought police' stifling discussion of all but state-approved topics and advocacy of all but the official position." So wrote Justice William Brennan in the dissenting opinion in a case that severely limits the right of students to express themselves freely in school.

In 1983, Cathy Kuhlmeier was student editor of *The Spectrum*, a newspaper published by the Journalism II class of Hazelwood East High School in a suburb of St. Louis, Missouri. The high school principal removed two pages from the May 13, 1983, issue of the newspaper without consulting the editors. The pages in question contained articles, including anecdotal and statistical data, on the subject of teenage pregnancy and the impact of divorce on children.

The principal claimed that the newspaper did not provide sufficient anonymity to a parent who was getting a divorce or to the three teenagers who were or had been pregnant. He objected to the favorable slant given to the subject of teenage pregnancy. He thought a column on birth control and sexual activity was inappropriate for younger students. A printing deadline, he claimed, made it impossible for him to consult with students about possible revisions.

By deleting the stories, the principal and other school administrators found themselves involved in a lawsuit that challenged the extent and limitations of press freedom in America. In court, the student editors charged that the principal's action amounted to press censorship and was in violation of the student editors' First Amendment rights. In 1985, a federal district judge ruled that the newspaper was merely a part of the journalism class and was, therefore, not an open forum entitled to the protection of the First Amendment.

In a 2-1 decision later that year, a three-judge panel of the U.S. Court of Appeals for the Eighth Circuit said that the student newspaper was entitled to protection under the First Amendment. In its decision, the court of appeals ruled that a student newspaper was "... a conduit for student viewpoint" and as such not merely a part of the curriculum.

To the great relief of school administrators, it was this decision that the United States Supreme Court reversed. In a 5-3 ruling, the court gave school administrators greater leeway to determine the contents of school newspapers. "A school need not tolerate student speech that is inconsistent with its basic educational mission," declared Justice Byron White in writing the majority opinion. "School officials," he continued, "may impose reasonable restrictions on the speech of students, teachers and other members of the school community."

Justice William Brennan (supported by Justices Marshall and Blackmun) wrote a scathing minority opinion. In it he said that the decision would make public schools "enclaves of totalitarianism ... that strangle the free mind at its source." Justice Brennan complained, "The young men and women of Hazelwood East expected a civics lesson, but not the one the court teaches today."

The fight for free speech is now in the hands of students like Cathy Kuhlheimer and other brave young journalists throughout the country. As Nat Hentoff wrote in *The First Freedom*, "If those Americans who are now in school do not come to see the First Amendment as a *personal* liberty, worth fighting for, then no written constitution can save it."

Twenty-five years ago, media expert Marshall MacLuhan anticipated the day when the world, which seemed enormous to our Founding Fathers, would shrink to become, in essence, a "global village." That day, it appears, has arrived. From high school newspapers to simultaneous international telecasts, the importance of free speech cannot be underestimated.

## The Global Village

In 1988, the Olympic games were held in Seoul, South Korea, but through electronic telecommunications, over two billion people participated in the excitement. And the same two billion people shared an incredible joy when, in the winter of 1989, the Berlin Wall came tumbling down. After 40 years living behind an Iron Curtain of silence, the people of Eastern Europe clamored to hear their own voices speak above the din of repression.

An Iron Curtain may no longer separate East and West. Competition in the form of a Cold War between capitalism and communism may not be as sharp as it once was. In the age of the electronic "global village," the challenge for today and tomorrow is how to extend the guarantees of the First Amendment to all peoples of the world.

If freedom of speech involves a "market place of ideas," as Justice Holmes said back in 1919, then today that marketplace is global in character.

To the extent that communications today are global, the information men and women need in order to make sensible choices in politics depends on the willingness of all nations to let that information flow freely across national boundaries.

Despite the recent, extraordinary achievements in Eastern Europe, this is not an easy goal to achieve. The United States has come closer to the goal of equal access to information than any nation in the world. Most nations have limited such access, sometimes endangering the entire earth with their restrictions. When a nuclear meltdown occurred in 1986 at Chernobyl, in the U.S.S.R., for instance, the failure of the Soviet government to notify immediately all other nations made the potential for disaster from radioactive fallout very real.

The global marketplace of ideas is also thwarted by the United Nations's attempt to limit what the world's people may read and see. The United Nations Education, Social and Cultural Organization (UNESCO) believes that access to information should be regulated and controlled. Most of the members, largely Third World or developing countries, insist that "cultural imperialism" from developed countries would subvert their own people and values. They worry that their populations will be unduly influenced by the western, mainly American, media. But other nations argue that the real worry is that the people will develop demands for higher living standards and popular participation in government. If knowledge is power, it will not be long before those with access to knowledge become more powerful than the governments that now control them.

The Third World countries are not wrong in recognizing that telecasts from the United States, for example, may encourage demands and attitudes that are unwelcome in authoritarian regimes. Yet unless the value of the free flow of information is reconciled with the value of limited access to information, freedom of expression in a global context is severely curtailed. Partly because of the attempt by UNESCO to inhibit a global free press, the United States dropped out of the organization in 1985.

An example of how media censorship in one country affects all countries may be found in the Union of South Africa. In 1985, the South African government made it illegal to show violent confrontation between blacks and whites in newspapers and on television. As a result, for the past several years, South Africans have received a distorted view of the progress of the fight against apartheid (racial separation) from their news sources. Moreover, censorship in South

Africa has tended to move the sensitive issue of apartheid to the back burner of television newscasts and newspapers. In a sense, if racial violence is not reported, the white minority of that country is able to strengthen its stranglehold on the reins of government and the channels of communication.

By encouraging *glasnost,* or a new openness at home and abroad, Soviet General Secretary Mikhail Gorbachev has encouraged a greater freedom of information between the Soviet Union and the United States. Several prominent weekly news magazines, such as *Time* and *Newsweek,* have begun negotiations toward an agreement to sell their journals in the U.S.S.R. An American book store will open in Moscow, where Russian-language editions of modern American classics will be published. Each nation has agreed to give the other the opportunity to challenge misconceptions or "disinformation" about its society. These are among the more important aspects of the new "global village" information exchange.

On January 6, 1941, as war clouds were gathering in Europe and Asia, President Franklin D. Roosevelt said, "In the future days, which we seek to make secure, we look forward to a world founded upon four essential freedoms. The first is freedom of speech and expression—everywhere in the world."[2] It's up to each and every one of us to keep striving to meet this lofty goal.

# Notes

Full source citations are listed in the Bibliography.

### CHAPTER ONE

1. Mill, 76.
2. Tocqueville, 95.
3. Swartz, 4.
4. Swartz, 15.
5. Tedford, 6.
6. Tedford, 7.

### CHAPTER THREE

1. Levy, 5.
2. Pfeffer, 71.
3. Sherrill, 25.
4. Jowett, 26.

### CHAPTER FOUR

1. Forer, 17.
2. Abram, 34.
3. Hentoff, 260.
4. Burke, 700.

### CHAPTER FIVE

1. Lieberman, 22.
2. *New York Times*, April 25, 1989.
3. Berns, 3-24.
4. Lapham, 34.

### CHAPTER SEVEN

1. Lieberman, 22.
2. Ernst.

# Bibliography

Abram, Floyd, "Why We Should Change the Libel Law." *New York Times Magazine* (September 29, 1985): 34.

Berns, Walter. "Democracy: The Case for Censorship." *The Public Interest* 22 (Winter, 1971): 3–24.

Bosmajian, Haig A., ed. *Freedom of Expression*. New York: Neal-Schuman, 1988.

Burke, John R. "Five Votes Shy of a Load: Reflecting on the Mass Media Today." *Vital Speeches* 51 (September 1, 1985): 700.

Ernst, Morris L. *The First Freedom*. New York: Macmillan, 1946.

Forer, Lois G. *A Chilling Effect*. New York: W. W. Norton, 1987.

Hentoff, Nat. *The First Freedom*. New York: Delacorte Press, 1980.

Jowett, Garth S. "The Selling of the Pentagon: Television Confronts the First Amendment." In *American History/American Television*, John E. O'Connor, ed. New York: Frederick Ungar, 1983.

Lapham, Lewis, ed. "The Place of Pornography." *Harper's* (November, 1984): 34.

Levy, Leonard, ed. *Freedom of the Press from Zenger to Jefferson*. New York: Bobbs-Merrill, 1966.

Lieberman, Jethro K. *Free Speech, Free Press and the Law*. New York: Lothrop, Lee and Sheppard, 1980.

Liebman, Morris I. "Second Lecture on Civil Disobedience." In William Sloane Coffin Jr. and Morris I. Liebman. Institute for Policy Research, 1972.

Mill, John Stuart. *On Liberty*. New York: Penguin Books 1974,

Pfeffer, Leo. *The Liberties of an American*. Boston: The Beacon Press, 1956.

Sherrill, Robert. "The Happy Ending (Maybe) of The Selling of the Pentagon." *New York Times Magazine* (May 16, 1971): 25.

Swartz, Bernard. *The Roots of the Bill of Rights*. New York: Chelsea House, 1980.

Tedford, Thomas. *Freedom of Speech in the United States*. New York: Random House, 1985.

Tocqueville, Alexis de. *Democracy in America*. New York: Washington Square Press, 1964.

# Suggestions for Further Reading

Bosmajian, Haig A., ed. *Freedom of Expression*. New York: Neal-Schuman, 1983.

This volume consists of selected cases involving the impact of Supreme Court decisions on students, teachers, administrators and schools.

Chafee, Zechariah, Jr. *Free Speech in the United States*. Cambridge, Massachusetts: Harvard University Press, 1941.

Although written almost 50 years ago, no reading list on freedom of expression could be complete without it. This is thoroughly readable, as only a preeminent scholar could make it.

Forer, Lois G. *A Chilling Effect*. New York: W. W. Norton, 1987.

The role of libel in America becomes lucid in this fine analysis.

Friendly, Fred W., and Martha J. H. Eliott. *The Constitution: That Delicate Balance*. New York: Random House, 1977.

This lively book is devoted to pivotal decisions that shaped freedom of expression in America.

Hentoff, Nat. *The First Freedom: The Tumultuous History of Free Speech in America*. New York: Dell, 1980.

This is a swiftly moving exposition of free speech written by a prominent journalist whose position is that any restraint on free speech is a threat to democracy.

Hook, Sidney. *The Paradoxes of Freedom*. Berkeley, California: University of California Press, 1962.

This distinguished philosopher discusses the extent and

limitations of freedom both in the abstract and the concrete.

Kalven, Harry, Jr. *A Worthy Tradition: Freedom of Speech in America*. New York: Harper and Row, 1988.
Modern interpretations of freedom of speech in America are the subject of this distinguished scholar's attention.

Neier, Aryeh. *Defending My Enemy: American Nazis, the Skokie Case and the Risks of Freedom*. New York: E. P. Dutton, 1979.
The son of Holocaust victims defends his role as director of the American Civil Liberties Union in protecting the rights of Nazis to demonstrate in Skokie, Illinois.

Pfeffer, Leo. *The Liberties of an American*. New York: The Beacon Press, 1956.
This account of First Amendment and other freedoms is written in nontechnical terms for a general audience.

Poole, Ithiel de Sola. *Technologies of Freedom*. Cambridge, Massachusetts: The Belknap of Harvard University, 1983.
This prominent scholar discusses the impact of new technologies on First Amendment and other freedoms.

Spitzer, Mathew L. *Seven Dirty Words and Six Other Stories*. New Haven: Yale University Press, 1986.
The impact on the broadcast media of the First Amendment is the subject of this volume.

## *INDEX*